HIDDEN QUESTIONS
CLINICAL MUSINGS

HIDDEN QUESTIONS
CLINICAL MUSINGS

M. Robert Gardner

Routledge
Taylor & Francis Group

LONDON AND NEW YORK

First published 1995 by The Analytic Press, Inc.

Published 2018 by Routledge
2 Park Square, Milton Park, Abingdon, Oxon, OX14 4RN
52 Vanderbilt Avenue, New York, NY 10017

First issued in paperback 2018

Routledge is an imprint of the Taylor & Francis Group, an informa business

Copyright © 1995 by Taylor & Francis.

Library of Congress Cataloging-in-Publication Data

Gardner, M. Robert
  Hidden questions, clinical musings / M. Robert Gardner
  p.   cm.
  Includes bibliographical references and index.
  ISBN 0-88163-212-0
  1. Psychoanalysis. I. Title.
RC509.G37 1995
616.89'17–dc20
DNLM/DLC
for Library of Congress   95-41685
                                                      CIP

Typeset by TechType, Upper Saddle River, NJ

The following chapters were published elsewhere and appear here, in slightly revised form and with some additions, by permission of their publishers: ch. 2–*Psychiatry Education Today,* by I. Hendrick (1965, International Universities Press); ch. 3–*International Journal of Psycho-Analysis* (1984, 65:39-44; ch. 4– Apres. Etudes (1984, No. 24); ch. 6–In *Self-Analysis: Critical Inquiries, Personal Visions* (1993, The Analytic Press); ch. 8–*Journal of the American Psychoanalytic Association* (1991, 39:851-870); ch. 10–*International Journal of Psycho-Analysis* (1994, 75:927-937).

ISBN 13: 978-1-138-87252-3 (pbk)
ISBN 13: 978-0-88163-212-5 (hbk)

CONTENTS

Preface   vii

1. A Busman's Holiday:
   A Psychiatrist Goes to the Barber   5

2. On Psychiatry and Other Schooling   9

3. Analysis and Self-Analysis:
   Looking Two Ways at Once   21

4. After?   34

5. To Be (Or Not to Be) An Analyst   48

6. On Talking to Ourselves: Some Self-Analytical
   Reflections on Self-Analysis   54

7. Recollections: Sexuality, Neurosis, and Analysis   76

8. The Art of Psychoanalysis:
     On Oscillation and Other Matters   100

9. And Who Will Analyze the Analysts?   122

10. Is That a Fact?: Empiricism Revisited,
      Or a Psychoanalyst at Sea   140

11. Free Association Revisited   162

References   183

Index   187

PREFACE

Any person who gives permission for the publication of a selection of his or her existing papers owes at least a brief explanation to anyone who might be expected to acquire, let alone read, it.

At first, I contemplated saying, "My editor made me." But that rang childish and untrue. And even if it had been more elderly and true, it appeared to offer insufficient justification for the deed in question. I thought then of seeking pardon on the grounds that only half the papers in this collection had earlier been published and one of those had been published only in French. But I decided at last to come straight to the point. I hope this collection may prove of interest to a person who likes to trace ways in which a few ideas—especially a few hidden questions—on one occasion or another press for expression, organization, and reorganization in the thinking and writings of a person who is possessed by and trying to take possession of those pressing ideas and questions.

To facilitate such tracings, I have tried retrospectively to annotate each paper. In that annotating, I have been reminded repeatedly of tensions that were lively in psychiatry and psychoanalysis when I was setting out. That is, I have been reminded in today's light of tensions I remember perceiving in yesterday's light, tensions that over the years since seem to have shaped persistently my evolving version of psychoanalysis and my periodical writings of clinical and extraclinical musings. To outline a few of those tensions, I have written this afterword that I now proffer as a foreword.

My earliest close encounters with analysts were not, by any ordinary standards, conspicuously close. When I was a medical student almost a half century ago, I drifted uninvited into a series of meetings — I believe they were called scientific — of the New York Psychoanalytic Society and of the Columbia Psychoanalytic Society. In those days, drifters were welcome. At least nobody said I was not. And those opportunities contributed significantly to the waning of my wish to become an internist and to the waxing of my wish to become an analyst. I remember two encounters in particular. And though I do not remember their chronological order, I remember the rank order I assigned.

First was an occasion on which Bert Lewin presented his paper on the dream screen. After that presentation, an aged, bearded gentleman arose from his seat — he looked exactly as I imagined an analyst should look — and pronounced the occasion momentous. He added wistfully that he wished Freud could have been present. I found it believable that this was a momentous occasion; and I found the yearning for Freud highly moving. I remember being particularly impressed that Lewin, by what seemed to me grand leaps of an artistic imagination, had arrived at the convincing conclusion that dreams, wishes, hopes, and breasts were inseparable. And this imaginative feat seemed to me very much in the literary tradition of the Freud I had read as an undergraduate.

The second of these memorable encounters was one at which Sandor Rado held forth. Rado spoke eloquently of the improvements that had come and were still to come; he spoke of making psychoanalysis more scientific. (I seem to recall that he pronounced it "see-entific.") He said that every intervention by an analyst was a scientific hypothesis and that its truth could be established only by extremely careful attention to a patient's subsequent responses. That seemed to me a praiseworthy departure from the authoritarian attitudes of which I had heard analysts accused. (Nor was I shaken from my enthusiasm for this scientific proposition by finding on this and later occasions that Rado usually spoke in a way that suggested he was not accustomed to speaking hypotheses.) Besides, I was further impressed when Rado spoke of the importance of avoiding terms that reflected or invited reification. And though I did not comprehend how not calling "The Unconscious" by that name and instead calling it "Nonreporting Consciousness" was going to prevent any ordinarily ingenious person from reifying it, I was impressed that Rado was giving it the old college try, a scientific college try. And I was impressed that psychoanalysis could make room for the artistic endeavors of a Lewin and the scientific endeavors of a Rado. (I make no claim to the accuracy of these designations; I am trying only to recount the impressions of a novice getting into position to make the decision to try to become a psychoanalyst.)

Contrasts never cease. A few years later, when I had become a resident at the New York State Psychiatric Institute, Nolan D. C. Lewis, director of the Institute, was fond of saying, "It's possible to be right and still be psychotic." I believe he was speaking mainly of paranoid patients, but his remark struck me as having much wider scope. Moreover, the spirit of his observation seemed very much in keeping with one of the contemporary preoccupations in that organization: the search for grounds on which to establish that some persons are much sicker than they seem. (This was, in particular, the era of pseudoneurotic schizophrenia.) Not long after, when I had become a resident at the Boston Psychopathic Hospital, I found myself facing a different preoccupation. Elvin Semrad seemed in many ways to be saying the opposite of what Nolan D. C. Lewis had said. Semrad seemed to be saying—and to be helping patients to demonstrate—that it's possible to be psychotic and still be right. And that is the first time I can remember being impressed that some propositions (especially, profound ones) read equally well backwards as forwards. Another momentous occasion. I can also remember wondering how best to blend Nolan D. C. Lewis's and Elvin Semrad's truths into an appropriate approach to patients.

Those were, for many reasons, heady days at the Boston Psychopathic Hospital, usually affectionately called "the Psycho." Everyone touted the virtues of a psychosomatic vision. "Psychosomatic" seemed to promise a long-lost vision of mind-body unity. But in the nitty gritty of their approaches to patients, some of my teachers seemed to favor disembodied psyche theories and therapies, and others, disenpsychied body theories and therapies. (This was the heyday of electroshock, insulin, lobotomy, and even a few experimental drops of LSD.) For my part, given the choice between mind and body, I opted without hesitation for mind. And that sealed my decision to become a psychoanalyst.

By far my most influential teacher at the Psycho was the always surprising Ives Hendrick. While others pulled one against the other, Hendrick, all by himself, seemed often to pull or be pulled in opposite directions. In his astute general discussions of the human condition, he talked often and persuasively of the importance of paying attention to matters preoedipal: to early identifications, to manifestations of the instinct to mastery, and so on. In his discussions of real live patients, however, he focused almost exclusively on matters oedipal. By the same token, he was strongly inclined toward hysterics. I remember a time he interviewed an elderly paranoid schizophrenic woman who seldom talked and, when she did, was invariably extremely hostile. Before long they were talking of the romances of her youth and then, in particular, of a romantic exchange with her first boy friend in the balcony of the local motion picture theater. I remember also that at the end of that interview, this woman, looking much younger and prettier, stood up and, after a conspicuous wiggle of her torso and a coquettish smile, thanked him warmly for seeing her. To this day, I remain convinced that she was thanking him for seeing her as a woman, and at that an hysteric rather than a paranoid schizophrenic. All of which spurred my interest— only years later recognizable—in the puzzling question of whether we can ever find anything except what we are looking for, and if so, how.

Soon after, I began my analytic schooling at the Boston Psychoanalytic Institute. Most of my teachers seemed to aim at, and often to attain, what in retrospect I regard as an admirably flexible classicism. But occasionally within that majority, and more often within a small but privately vociferous minority, the more extreme positions I perceived, or imagined, seemed continuations of the positions I had perceived, or imagined, in my aforementioned first forays into the psychiatric and psychoanalytic worlds. That is, some positions seemed to continue and extend those with which I was already familiar; a few seemed new; and a few, a blend of the old and the new.

Some positions were called classical. Others were called flexible. I cannot remember any of the more zealous adherents of either position ever expounding their positions in groups larger than two or three. And even in groups of two or three, it was, to the best of my recollection, never done stridently. This was a very "civilized" organization. Nevertheless, those who managed to convey most forcefully, if discreetly and relatively privately, that they were classical with a capital C, or flexible with a capital F managed not infrequently to do so in ways that suggested that one was incompatible with the other. Indeed, a few of the Classical positions seemed to border on orthodoxy; and one conspicuously strong case of Flexibility seemed to qualify as a new orthodoxy.

I do not suggest that this organization was built on a foundation of grossly transparent and easily resolvable contradictions. By and large, the positions of my teachers seemed sophisticated, judicious, and compelling. Which made them, for a novice, even more confusing. I recall Helen Tartakoff, for example, making a highly responsible and persuasive case for limiting psychoanalysis to patients for whom it was especially suited. I recall others making equally responsible and persuasive cases for what Leo Stone called "the widening scope."

And some positions seemed to overlap these widening or nonwidening positions. Elizabeth Zetzel, for one, had begun to elaborate on the importance of "building a therapeutic alliance." I was impressed by her efforts to encourage a reasonable adaptability in our dealings with patients – the "sicker" patients and the less – and especially her efforts to expose our misunderstandings of analytic "neutrality," of the "imposing of abstinence," of the oft-recommended eschewing of early transference interpretation, and of other rules of thumb that threatened to become arthritic. By all this and more, I was much impressed.

Occasionally, however, in discussing the "building of a therapeutic alliance," Zetzel would suggest such measures as saying "we" to the patient or would suggest other measures that struck me as falling into the category of How to Win Friends and Influence People. More often, these oddities were advanced by analysts or analysts-to-be who, though claiming to follow Zetzel's lead in building alliances, seemed more intent on building unholy alliances. Accordingly, I could appreciate the position of vociferous others who said there was absolutely no necessity to "build" an alliance, that an alliance would develop spontaneously if an analyst simply properly did his or her job, and that efforts to "build" an alliance were bound to lead to mésalliance. Indeed, it had already become apparent, to those of us of little experience, that the notion of "building" an alliance was being misused by some analysts to rationalize peculiar activities called "showing that the analyst is human" or in some cases "showing that the analyst is real." (I am not sure whether "human" and "real" were synonymous or had slightly different connotations.) I cannot say exactly what I learned from that long ago and faraway strife over whether or not to "build." But, as I look back today, I believe the tensions reflected in the positions of the builders and the nonbuilders, and in the positions of those who claimed to – or even seemed to – rise easily above the fray, intensified my growing preoccupations with, and hidden questions about, the self-analytical and other measures needed within the framework of an analysis to find respectful ways to reach out to patients.

These, then, were a few of the questions—some manifest, most hidden—that, four or five decades ago, faced my analytic friends and me, questions of whether we find only what we are looking for (or occasionally find something else), whether the widening scope of analysis is a blessing or a misfortune, whether to build or not to build an alliance, whether analysis is art or science, whether patients are sicker or healthier than they seem, whether mind can be reunited with body, whether exploration of mainly one sector of development constitutes a proper parsimony or a regrettable rigidity, whether 'tis better to frame analytic observations and theories in one language or another, and whether one language is, on the average or at any one moment, any less reifiable than another. There were more. But these were enough for a start.

As I look back at the years that followed, it seems to me that those questions in one form or another—some manifest, most hidden—have stayed with me ever since. I believe they have moved me to pay fuller attention both to them and to other of my questions (manifest and hidden), to my patients' questions (manifest and hidden), to the play between my patients' questions and mine, and to the forces that organize and are organized by such questions and such play. These heightenings of attention seem to have led over time—I believe they have led me more than I have led them—to the changes in my ways of trying to help patients and myself to explore surfaces and depths, and to the changes in my visions of the workings of the mind, that emerge gradually in the papers in this collection. If any of the tensions and questions with which I have struggled, and if any of the paths they have invited, urged, or obliged me to walk, resemble those of anyone else, then perhaps these papers will prove of interest.

HIDDEN QUESTIONS
CLINICAL MUSINGS

Correspondences

Nature's a temple where the pilasters
Speak sometimes in their mystic languages;
Man reaches it through symbols dense as trees,
That watch him with a gaze familiar

As far-off echoes from a distance sound
In unity profound and recondite,
Boundless as night itself and as the light,
Sounds, fragrances, and colours correspond.

Baudelaire

═══════════════════════

Chapter One

A BUSMAN'S HOLIDAY
A Psychiatrist Goes to the Barber

My barber's name is Charlie. When Charlie cuts hair he talks. He talks freely. Each time I sit down, Charlie says, "Well, Doc, no sign of baldness yet. Looks pretty thick. Wish I had hair like that."

Charlie always says that. One day, after the usual, Charlie went on:

"What do you think of Harvard, Doc? Just can't seem to get started. I don't know what'sa matter. They used ta win 'em all. Anyway, most of 'em. Six, seven a year. In the old days.

"Had a lotta trouble last week, Doc. Eye trouble. Got somethin in my right eye, not too bad, so I go to the drug store and he can't do nothin so I go to the emergency room at the General and this intern starts fishin around, it musta been an hour, and then he says he ain't sure if he's got it out and I should come back if it bothers me. Jeez. So he puts this big bandage on me and I go home and when I get to my block I take it off cause I don't wanna worry the little woman. Ya know. But when I get in, she knows all about it cause this neighbor sees me in the street and tells her all about it. Ya can't win. The whole damn neighborhood knows. The missus makes me put the bandage back on and she keeps fussin about it and I say, ' Look, it ain't nuttin. Just a little thing. Stop worryin.' But you know how women are, Doc. She keeps fussin and fussin as if it wuz somethin.

"She's the same way, the kid cuts his finger. He's a demon. Always inta somethin. The other day, he needed seven stitches. I told the missus it wuz nuttin. She keeps fussin. He's some tough kid though. Always inta somethin. One night he gets up and starts playin wit his flashlight. Runnin all over the place. Puts this big sheet on and jumps out at his sister. She screams bloody murder. I unnerstan. I was the same way when I wuz a kid. But ya gotta crack down on em. I takes my hair brush and I put it to him. Not too hard. Just a little.

"My old man was a barber too, ya know. He sure couldn't see it when I said I wanna be barber. I jus got back from Service and wanna settle down. He says, 'A barber? No. A man comes over from Italy. He can be a barber. That's good. A man is born here, he can be anything. Not a barber—a lawyer, a doctor, anything.' I told him, 'No. A barber is good enough for me.'

"Ya know, Doc, a barber has gotta supply his own stuff. Scissors. Combs. Everything. Some people don' know that."

When Charlie finishes cutting my hair, he says, "Well, Doc, that oughta pass inspection. See what the wife thinks. She'll like it. The women always know." And then he says, "Have a good weekend, Doc." Charlie always says that about the inspection, my wife, and having a good weekend.

Another time, Charlie said, "Well, Doc, no sign of baldness yet. Looks pretty thick. Wish I had hair like that," and then he went on:

"Whadda ya think of this Anastasia business? Musta been Costello. Ya think? Howdaya like that guy? Probly like you and me. Coulda gone inta a respectable business. Just went the udder way. Then, poof it's all over. Just like that. Ya hear about how it happened? He's sittin in a barber chair. One guy comes in on one side. One guy comes in on the udder. They push the barber aside—they let him have it. Right in the chair. Fill him fulla lead. Jus' like that.

"I seen a lot of blood growin up. Hell of a lot. No exaggeratin, Doc. Seen four differen' guys get shot. Jeez. How da ya like dat Anastasia? Pumped him full a lead.

"Ya know, Doc, I got a little trouble in my elbow dese days, the right one. Kinda sharp pain. Not alla time. Sometimes. When I move it too much. Whadda ya think? Bursitis maybe? Say, what's bursitis anyway? I'd hate ta have anything really wrong. I get it up bout this high and it starts to hurt.

"Hey, I jus got an idea, Doc. Whadda ya say I brush it up here like this? See how it looks. Pretty good, huh? That's how ya oughta do it, Doc. Looks great. Up like dis. Ya see? It fills in that, uh, uh, lil hollow place. We let it grow a lil longer here and nobuddy'll know what it covers. Ya can do yaself evry mornin. Train it up like dat. Funny I never thought of dat before. Yeah. That's great. You'll be a reglar movie star, Doc. Me, I'd need stilts. But one time I saw George Raft right up close. Jeez, he's no bigger than me.

"Well that oughta do it, Doc. Pass inspection. See what ya wife thinks. The women always know."

And then he said, "Have a great weekend, Doc."

AFTERTHOUGHTS

This previously unpublished piece was written in 1957. It was set down in my journals in a collection of entries called "Free Associations of Everyday Life." My original intention was to combine those entries into a book. "Charlie," however, is the sole survivor of periodic housecleanings.

Following "Charlie" are a few cryptic comments about his concern with "hidden damage," his compensatory tonsorial activities, and his tensions between friendly and hostile intentions toward his father and his customers. Those comments are followed by several cryptic questions: "Why is Charlie talking standing up as if he were talking lying down? Does Charlie know I'm a psychiatrist? If so, is that why he is talking as if he were a patient lying down and I a psychiatrist seated behind? Is Charlie only driven or is Charlie driving at something?"

That last question—"Is Charlie only driven or is Charlie driving at something?"—could have served as the title of this current collection. I gather I was wondering about the immediate organizers—inquisitive organizers—of Charlie's apparent outpourings from his depths. I gather, that is, that I was wondering what Charlie was wondering. My latent preoccupation with ways in which we are at once both driven and driving—and with the hidden questions that reflect the tensions between the two—appears, or almost appears, then disappears, then reappears, or almost reappears, throughout this present collection till it becomes, after many years, a manifest preoccupation.

Chapter Two

ON PSYCHIATRY
AND OTHER SCHOOLING

In 1917 Alfred North Whitehead reminded the Mathematical Association of England that mathematics is a science and that education in mathematics should be a scientific education. He defined scientific education as

> a training in the art of observing natural phenomena and in the knowledge and deduction of laws concerning the sequence of such phenomena. . . . There are many types of natural phenomena and to each type there corresponds a science with its peculiar modes of observation and its peculiar types of thought employed in the deduction of laws.

Many of us here today believe that psychiatry is sufficiently peculiar to justify its inclusion as a science, or, as Dr. Hendrick terms it, a basic science. Mr. Whitehead had a special interest in what he called the rhythm of education, the sequences and duration of stages in learning. He said, "Different subjects and modes of study should be undertaken by pupils at fitting times when they have reached the proper stage of development." He continues, "You will agree with me that this is a truism never doubted and known to all, but I do not think this obvious truth has been handled in educational practice with due attention to the psychology of the pupils."

I mention Mr. Whitehead to stress that the problems of teachers in other disciplines are not entirely different from those of teachers of psychiatry, and to stress another obvious truth: that the first concern of any teacher—and I think this applies as much in the arts as the sciences—is to foster observation and the understanding of what is observed.

All of us who have shared in the "Psycho" experience have shared in a tradition of disciplined exploration. This tradition seems to me to distinguish a first-rate educational institution from an information center. The major concern of those who have honored this tradition has not been with pontificating abstractions nor with dispensing rules of thumb for the do-it-yourselfer but with learning and teaching the basic moves: the methods of observing, the ways of organizing observations, and the ways of understanding the relationships of the observed phenomena. I believe this is not simply adherence to a principle of psychiatric education or even of scientific education, but adherence to a principle of any education. Whether there is a general recognition that science is more than physical science, that psychiatry is or can be basic science, does not concern me so deeply as an acceptance of the right and obligation of workers in any field to observe and think about their observations in ways useful to this field, no matter how bizarre or confusing the particular modes may seem to those who work in other fields.

There is some evidence that in actual practice in psychiatric education we do not always live up to our high ideals and sometimes work directly counter to them.

Dr. Hendrick has presented in detail his observations of the current psychiatric scene and his recommendations for the improvement of psychiatric education. In discussing his comments, I cannot possibly do justice to the breadth or the depth of his presentation, but I know that Dr. Hendrick will want us to say what we think of a few of his ideas and not simply to treasure them all as beautiful packages not to be opened until some future date.

Dr. Hendrick has made a number of points about research. Since this is a charged subject, perhaps it is a good place to start. Dr. Hendrick speaks of a peril that confronts psychiatry, that is, the spreading idea that the future of psychiatry as a science depends chiefly on laboratories, statistics, or the social sciences. He offers some evidence that this attitude is widespread and perhaps on the increase. I am not sure of the general prevalence or rate of growth, but I can say that antipsychological and anticlinical attitudes seem common not only outside of psychiatry, but among persons who call themselves clinicians in the ranks of eclectic psychiatry, dynamic psychiatry, and psychoanalysis. And, yet along with this, there seems to be another development, the appearance of a number of laboratory workers, statisticians, and social scientists struggling to gain an appreciation of the potentialities and limits of their own fields and of clinical psychiatry. I also see psychiatrists, clinical and nonclinical, involved in an effort to understand the value and limits of the clinical approach and of the methods of the laboratory workers, statisticians, and social scientists. Efforts of those in each group may eventually provide a better atmosphere for work, an atmosphere in which there is less tendency to sanctify or ritualize formal psychotherapy, or the statistical approach, or the social sciences, or the physical laboratory. In keeping with this, I think a case can be made for participation of a psychiatrist, at some point in this education, in interdisciplinary research. I see this as an effort to understand techniques of observation that may not be appropriate to or possible within the clinical setting and to grasp something of the uniqueness of clinical possibilities, that is, to see through experience that there are special opportunities for observation and study within the clinical setting and special opportunities in other settings. I say this with considerable bias in favor of the clinical approach as the basic approach to be learned by all psychiatrists. But I think the primary contribution of research in the early years of education should be a contribution to the development of a sounder appreciation of the potential of clinical and nonclinical work, and of psychological and nonpsychological approaches.

Much as I would hope that resident participation in research could make this contribution, I have found that this is not the case. Early exposure to work on an interdisciplinary team or to nonpsychological or nonclinical research does not appear to me to lead to such desirable developments but to have quite opposite effects. There is the matter of dissipation of energy to which Dr. Hendrick has already called attention. There is another problem. The resident who does not have sufficient clinical and psychological experience tends, when he participates in research, to see the clinical and the nonclinical, the psychological and the nonpsychological, as antagonistic. This may be reinforced by the reality of conflicting time demands and by the reality of conflicting demands of antagonistic teachers. Residents involved in research in their early years seem to become swept up in an increasing process of overrating the nonclinical and nonpsychological and downgrading the psychological and clinical, or to become defensively preoccupied with proving the superiority of clinical and psychological methods yet unlearned and with devaluing other methods. The peculiar paradoxical effect of too early concentration on team research is a strengthening of the wall between clinical and nonclinical and between psychological and nonpsychological workers.

As for the early participation of residents in research in clinical work, and in particular in psychotherapy, this seems to deteriorate in most instances into a stereotyped preoccupation with one detail of psychotherapy at the expense of a grasp of the real complexity of the situation. In other cases it becomes the vehicle for undisciplined technical innovations in an attempt to improve methods that have not yet been learned. Surely a resident may do genuinely creative and original work, but a one-sided preoccupation with creativity and originality may interfere seriously with learning in general and with the delicate interplay of discipline and spontaneity necessary for creative effort. The rush to communicate the first casual observations and to preserve these for posterity in the form of a paper, often the first of a series of papers announcing the intention to study the facts more carefully tomorrow, seems to be one of the occupational diseases of our field. The predisposition to this disease may be seriously increased by an exaggerated stress on research in the early years of the psychiatrist's education.

I do not know what constitutes too early or too intense involvement in research. What is too early and too intense for some residents may not be so for others. I urge serious consideration of the proposal to postpone formal research in most cases until after the second or third year of clinical experience. There are those who fear that if the resident is not exposed early to formal research that he will spend his career in a clinical ivory tower dully repeating the dogma and rituals of his predecessors. It is not, I think, sound clinical work that threatens progress; but not the least of the real threats to progress is the sanctification of the clinical by some and of the nonclinical by others, and the early enlistment of the resident in a destructive holy war.

Dr. Hendrick has spoken of the effects of premature exposure of medical students and residents to theoretical abstraction, and, I would add, to second-hand observation—in short, the tendency of a small dose of attenuated information, along with the booster effects of some kinds of teaching, to serve as an effective vaccine against direct observation and learning. Undoubtedly, the curricula of residency, of medical school, of college, and even of secondary and primary school are involved. Premature exposure to the theoretical abstractions of psychiatry and to second-, third-, and fourth-hand observations is more than a curriculum problem; it is a fact of life. Today everybody psychologizes. Psychological cliche and pseudoobservation are, of course, not mid-20th-century inventions. But pseudoanalysis and quasi-technical jargon are enjoying a remarkable vogue in all spheres of everyday life. Many students come to psychiatry today burdened by considerable exposure to and skill at explaining psychological phenomena without observing.

Today most students do not come to psychiatry as pioneers exploring an uncharted wilderness; they come loaded down with instructions, with guide books, and with a considerable number of organized preconceptions, some valuable, some not so valuable, many of them accumulated over a lifetime. It is very hard in such circumstances to see the view. I am not now referring to specific neurotic obstacles to the practice of observation in our field. I am suggesting the necessity of student and teacher recognizing and trying to free the student of the effects of long exposure to and practice in shallow psychologizing. By student I mean the student who is called student and the student who is called teacher; for in some cases the exchange between student and teacher is marred by the powerful mutual tendency toward exchange of increasingly sophisticated clichés—a sharing in a conventionally correct but empty discussion.

Premature abstraction and pseudoobservation are, I think, problems inherent in the present age of psychiatry, and the particular problems of this age are reflected in many of the practices Dr. Hendrick has described. In an age of popularity, new insights are easily disposed of by translation into clichés. Some of the most important insights in psychiatry seem to have been disposed of in this fashion already. The difficult task of the student of any era, but particularly of the modern student of psychiatry, is not only to pioneer at the frontier but to pioneer in rediscovering, in finding the truth in truism, in paying serious attention to the obvious. Rediscovery is a very demanding venture, in some ways harder than other forms of pioneering.

I think the practical implementation of the aims of discovery and rediscovery lies in an increased stress on direct observation and on its methods. Some teachers and students can achieve this emphasis in the context of discussions of psychotherapy. As a student and teacher, I have found that the diagnostic interview provides a freer atmosphere of exchange for most students and teachers. This appears to be true both in the first and in subsequent years of psychiatric education. Without minimizing the worth of appropriate supervision in psychotherapy, I would like to say something in favor of more extensive use of careful diagnostic work in psychiatric education, work undertaken not simply as a hurdle to be jumped on the way to therapy, but as an extremely rewarding learning experience in itself. Unfortunately, diagnostic interviewing is easily associated with a cold, mechanical pursuit of facts and may, for this reason, to say nothing of the amount of work involved, be avoided. Good diagnostic work can make a contribution to dispelling the curious notion that paying attention to people is being neglectful. I believe the emphasis on developing observational skill should be pursued vigorously throughout a psychiatrist's formal education and the years to follow.

I particularly want to express my agreement with Dr. Hendrick that to learn to make clinical decisions, so-called administrative decisions, without careful study and dynamic understanding of the needs of the individual is to learn to practice poor psychiatry. Dynamic understanding should not be confined to a psychotherapeutic hothouse.

I would like to turn now to the matter of the resident's heavy involvement in technical tasks within the early years of his education and his tendency to become heavily involved in off-duty tasks, including the private practice of psychotherapy. I shall consider one aspect.

Today a student undergoes many pressures to get on with the job of applying the insights of his field to pressing advanced technical problems—in therapy, in research, in administration, in public health, in politics, and in other areas. From within and outside his educational institution, he is offered substantial rewards in the form of status, money, and, what is probably most seductive to a serious student, the chance to broaden his experience. If participation in some of these activities is arranged with serious attention to the demands of education, this can be an effective part of an educational program. Few of us today would aim at the Platonic ideal of complete separation of learning and doing. Least of all would this be acceptable in psychiatry. But extensive and early participation in complex and demanding technical activities calls for repeated careful scrutiny to be sure that these in fact enhance education. Whatever the advantages of these activities, they pose a particular problem. If novices are assigned to advanced technical tasks at the outset of the first year, it should come as no great surprise if they tend to leap rapidly into similar tasks outside the hospital in the second and third year. For the resident this may be a logical though not necessarily wise extension. I think one of the major arguments against the resident's assuming excessive responsibility early in his career, in the hospital or outside, is that it forces premature acquisition of skills that may in the long run interfere with his full growth and development—a problem not unknown in the arts and in the world of sports, to mention but two examples. There may be good reasons for ignoring optimum pace, but it is a serious matter. The almost successful methods forged in these early fires are hard to recognize and harder to unlearn.

This matter of the resident's busyness, to which Dr. Hendrick has referred, has another aspect. Many are on their way to subspecialization usually involving a long, arduous, and expensive effort. There is the risk that the period of basic education may be experienced as an unfortunate delay in the march to child psychiatry, psychosomatic medicine, psychoanalysis, administration, research, and so on. Under such circumstances, it is easy to become very busy in the early years, not with basic education, but in activities that seem to relate more directly to long-range aims. There is a parallel observable in our universities, where teachers have become alert to the need for constant enrichment and improvement of the undergraduate program to overcome the tendency of student and teacher alike to see the undergraduate program as less important than the graduate programs. There is also an unfortunate tendency for some teachers to recruit students for postgraduate work by premature stress on the techniques and ideas of their particular subspecialized fields. An educational program developed by a group of subspecialists can easily become a well-rounded smattering of previews, ensuring that the student is too busy to get the hang of anything.

Whatever our problems in psychiatric education, I have the impression that we have a special advantage, and that is that most of our students and our teachers are deeply imbued with that urge to explore to which Dr. Hendrick has referred. I think most students, given sufficient chance, can assess what it is that cannot be used and must, at least for the time being, be discarded. But this takes time, and it takes an intense involvement of student and teacher. Short of this, the student may carry away a fabric of slogans and tricks of the trade useful for identifying himself as a member of this or that coterie, or the student successfully avoids any involvement at all; in either case, he does not go with the basic necessities for future growth and development. Too many subjects and too many teachers means exposure to more and more of less and less. Under these circumstances, the valuable urge to explore can become an anxious concern with being up to date, an exaggerated emphasis on latest theoretical extensions and revisions, an agitated romp from one teacher to another, one journal to another, one conference to another, one institution to another, ad infinitum. Different in form but equally destructive is the development of a student who decides this is all nonsense and retires into seclusion rationalized as a neoclassical revival, uncontaminated by the tawdry facts of contemporary life.

We have, in the main, a good subject. We have good students, and we have good teachers. If we are clear on our basic aim of trying to understand human beings in human terms, if we do not try to learn or to teach too much too quickly, if we are not floored by our rapid transition from hermit to life of the party, if we organize our teaching programs with sufficient involvement of student, fellow student, and a few teachers, I think psychiatry will fare quite well.

I was surprised by Dr. Hendrick's reference to the possibility that the guiding principle of dynamic psychiatry in psychiatric education may some day disappear as the Hudson River does out in the Atlantic. Perhaps it is true that dynamic psychiatry will ultimately disappear as an entity, but I suspect that, though at the moment it seems to be disappearing forever, it is, at its source, just beginning.

<hr/>

AFTERTHOUGHT

Hendrick's paper and my discussion were a portion of a program on October 13, 1962 to celebrate the 50th anniversary of what had been the Boston Psychopathic Hospital and had since been renamed the Massachusetts Mental Health Center. (The abiding principle of nomenclature seemed to be that one bad name deserves another.) Both Hendrick's (1965) paper and my discussion (Gardner, 1965) were subsequently published.

Hendrick began by highlighting his conviction that dynamic psychiatry is a basic science. He went on to specify some ways in which a basic science needs teaching. He was especially at pains to stress the risks of teaching dynamic psychiatry—or any other science—in ways that "subordinate hard clinical effort to facile abstraction." For my part, I was not so sure that dynamic psychiatry was best classified as a science. It seemed to me to follow in some regard the aims and means of the sciences and in some, those of the arts. But I was in agreement that dynamic psychiatry, whether a science or an art or moving somewhere between, was best seen as a unique ("peculiar") way of observing psychological events, of discerning the patterns they form, and of organizing and trying to account for those patterns. And I was in agreement that dynamic psychiatry should be taught with appropriate emphasis on its special methods, not as a set of "facile abstractions."

The context of our agreement, and my tangentially expressed disagreement, was that Hendrick was highly concerned about present and potential dilutions of teaching. He regarded these as stemming from a failure to recognize that dynamic psychiatry is a science. For my part, I was of the opinion that the excellence of the teaching program that Hendrick had developed was more despite, than because of, his insistence that dynamic psychiatry is a science. To the degree I shared his concern about threatened dilution I was more concerned about the risks, present and potential, of efforts to dignify dynamic psychiatry and psychoanalysis by aping the forms and language of science—of some sciences—in ways that seemed to me to qualify more as scientism than science and therefore to demean what they purported to dignify and to compress and distort dynamic psychiatry and psychoanalysis to fit distorted visions of science. (The subtext of this agreement and disagreement was that Hendrick had managed, in considerable part by his insistence that dynamic psychiatry was a basic science, to sell his program of teaching to the powers that governed the Harvard Medical School. As a junior member of the staff, and of this public celebration, I was not about to press, in more than passing reference, my doubts about those grounds for claiming legitimacy.

Hendrick closed his remarks by expressing the concern that dynamic psychiatry had already begun to undergo a dilution and some day would disappear "as the Hudson River disappears into the Atlantic." Nowadays, his remarks about the fate of dynamic psychiatry, at least in Boston, might seem to have been prescient. But being young and enthusiastic, I was concerned to balance what seemed to me Hendrick's gloomy prediction with a more optimistic one, that is, to balance a judicious pessimism with a judicious optimism. Which led me to respond: "Perhaps it is true that dynamic psychiatry will ultimately disappear as an entity, but I suspect that, though at the moment it seems to be disappearing forever, it is, at its source, just beginning."

Hendrick and I were both former New Yorkers. Over the years we had talked often of our love for the Hudson and its surround. (He often said that if things got any worse he could always return to New York and drive a cab.) Accordingly, our Hudson play in this program was dear to us both. And I did think that, although he might be correct about a bout of doom and gloom in the short run, he was probably wrong about the long. In retrospect, I think my concluding silver-lining-ish remark reflected a broader and longer preoccupation with appearances, disappearances, and reappearances of constructive currents, a preoccupation that later takes the shape of a preoccupation with hidden questions and other forward flows, which, having long antedated the occasion at hand and having recently cropped up evanescently in Charlie the Barber, then subsequently appears, disappears, and reappears in various ways in various essays to come.

Chapter Three

ANALYSIS AND SELF-ANALYSIS
Looking Two Ways at Once

W henever one analyst tells his or her work to another, it is tempting to the told analyst to tell the telling analyst what the telling analyst might have seen, could have seen, should have seen, might have done, could have done, should have done. When the tale is as vivid and as gripping as Dr. Spruiell's, the grand illusion of our being there, and the temptation to do the analyst's job, is still greater. At least, it is for me.

But there is and can be, in one analysis, but one analyst. I think De Tocqueville would have been pleased to discover that even in the United States analysis is not done by committee. Each analyst is, for better and for worse, an original. I do not analyze the way Dr. Spruiell does. Dr. Spruiell does not analyze the way I do. We are all, whether of the same school or not, the same predilections or not, more different than alike. Yet whether or not of different predilections, different schools, and different nations, we are, insofar as we are all analysts, all countrymen.

Though it might be interesting to explore our considerable differences, I believe that the delineation of difference may prove more fruitful if it follows, or at least accompanies, the delineation of likeness. Beginning with that assumption, I hope to consider some ways in which Dr. Spruiell and the rest of us, despite our considerable differences, might conceivably be considered countrymen.

I have organized my remarks with regard to, and with respect for, his admirable departure from those conventions of reporting in which the analyst is portrayed as perfect observer and perfect analyzer. I shall isolate a few fragments of the analysis, speculate about them, and then try to say what I think Dr. Spruiell helps us most particularly to see of ourselves, of our ways of working, and of ways we might possibly work better.

For a point of departure and a frame of reference, I want to underscore Dr. Spruiell's comment on the aim of psychoanalysis: "Psychoanalysis," he says, "is the analysis of one mind, as far as the psychoanalysis can take it, without the analyst attempting to take over responsibility for parts of that mind or its concerns outside the analytic situation."

That seems to me an acceptable version of our analyzing ideal. It may ask a great deal but then so does anything worthy of the name "ideal."

Each of us, in his or her own way, could restate that ideal. We could narrow it in some ways, broaden it in others. We could spell out in our different ways what we mean by "analyze" and by "mind," and how, in this regard, we see the play of what we call "understanding" and what we call "experiencing" in the analytic endeavor. We could stress "conflict," and one or another aspect of "conflict," and/or a broader range of human dilemmas. We could assign different values to the analysis of the here-and-now: whether the transference, the resistance, the character, or other lively interplays of past and present.

A brief survey of even these few considerations would

probably produce much grist for the mills of discussion and debate, but more grist, perhaps, than we can currently mill. Yet I think we could agree that we all try in our various ways, and in accord with our various interests and theories, to do what Dr. Spruiell says: to analyze as much as we can what we regard as workings of the mind and not to usurp responsibility.

Let me elaborate a bit what I imagine he and we have in mind:

We have positive analyzing aims, variously defined; we have negative analyzing aims, variously defined. We try to facilitate—at least not to impede—the growth of our patients; we try not to push that growth. We try to help our patients to analyze the workings of their minds; we try not to intrude upon those workings. We try to help our patients to expand their abilities to explore their minds; we try not to insist too doggedly or exclusively on our own ways of exploring. We try to make some choices more possible; we try not to force the time or particulars of choice.

Moreover, when we invite attention to how our patients think, feel, perceive, and act, we try not to suggest or to imply that *any* working of the mind is necessarily, in the short run or the long, exclusively harmful or useful, wrong or right, destructive or creative. Aware of the ubiquity—and searching for the particulars—of multiple function, and of what we might call multiple consequence, we try to maintain (or to achieve) a proper respect for our patients' complexities. And though we all have our manifest or latent expectations of what we regard desirable change (some call it "health"; others find such designation entirely too medicinal), we all, nevertheless, regard it best to confine ourselves, insofar as we can, to analyzing the workings of the mind. We are of good faith (or try to be) that favorable changes will best occur in response to our patients' thrusts toward development, not pressures from us. We try to find common ground for our patients' agendas of inquiry and our own. All this and more in our analyzing stance we refer to by that curious term: neutral.

But, as Dr. Spruiell reminds us, what we hold ideal and what we actually do are not, and cannot be, in simple or full harmony. Sometimes we are unable to live up; and sometimes, as the old saying goes, we must rise above our ideals and do the right thing. And often the distinction between failing and rising above is distressingly unclear.

Take, for example in this analysis, the battle of the pot, the battle, that is, over marijuana and other drugs. The patient's use of drugs—"dependency on drugs"—produced serious problems for the analysis. We do not know in detail what they were, but let's accept that there were problems, that they were serious, and that stopping the use of the drugs seemed critical to continuing the analysis. The analyst, therefore, after trying other measures, told the patient, at last, that he "would not continue [the analysis] unless [the patient] agreed to stop the use of drugs absolutely."

I realize that Dr. Spruiell may not have given an exact quote of what he said, but permit me to treat it as being, in spirit, exact. The patient must agree not only to stop, but "to stop absolutely." That is the difference, I suppose, between the signs on New Hampshire highways that say "Speed Limit: 55 MPH" and those that say "Absolute Speed Limit: 55 MPH." There is a certain extra force in the "absolutely."

There is also the force that comes not simply from the suggestion that stopping drugs might be useful to the analysis, but from the threat that the consequences of not stopping—stopping absolutely—will be a stopping of the analysis. There is probably the force that comes from a note of exasperation in the injunction. There is surely the force of history: the special impact on a man whose clinging to drugs was said to be preceded by a prolonged clinging to his mother, and whose experience of a force from behind was said to have been preceded by special force from behind in earlier battles of opposition and endearment. There is, too, the impact of the threat of abandonment in a man who reports that his parents "vanished" without warning when he was five. (In this last regard, there is both the threat of a terrible repetition of history and the possibility of a new and better ending: this time, he *has* a warning and he has the chance, by however painful, and pleasurable, a submission, to prevent the vanishing of the analyst.)

We can readily appreciate Dr. Spruiell's quandary. He would prefer not to play out all this. But he can find no alternative. We all know that quandary. Our ideal is to analyze the workings of our patient's mind and not to take responsibility for the workings or the choices. Yet sometimes we judge it necessary to exercise pressure that frustrates or pressure that gratifies, or that, seeming to frustrate, also gratifies, or that, seeming to gratify, also frustrates. Whether Dr. Spruiell might have chosen another way is not what I want now to address. In one voice, we might say he could have set forth his injunction sooner. In another, we might say he could have done it later, or not at all.

In the years since this incident, he, and we, *may* have developed methods that *might* have made the injunction—or its particular form or force—unnecessary. The history of an individual analyst often recapitulates the history of our field in the slow but steady expansion of ways to advance exploratory aims and means and to curtail the prescriptive and proscriptive. An individual analyst's progress in any particular analysis often follows the same sequence.

Meanwhile, we do what we can. More often than not, we depart a bit, or a lot, from our analyzing ideals. I am speaking of departures small or large, direct or indirect, good, bad, or indifferent, departures of mixed motives and mixed consequences. I want to mention this matter of mixed motive and mixed consequence now and come back to it soon.

Meanwhile, consider the moment. The analyst, after much soul-searching, has taken a position: an "absolute" position. He has asked his patient to discontinue one time-worn pattern (drugtaking). Ironically, in the doing, he has asked him to continue another: to play, that is, what he later recognizes as Ganymede to Jove.

We all know this dilemma. We know it well, in analysis and elsewhere. Setting out to do one thing, we do another. Setting out with one intention, we unintentionally, and with intentions we do not yet know, do another.

Nor are such dilemmas confined to those moments when we wrestle long and self-consciously with whether or not, or how, to issue an injunction. At the risk of documenting the obvious, I invite you to consider another incident:

The patient began an hour by telling that in a delicatessen near the place of his analysis, he thought it would be interesting to bring to his analyst, in a styrofoam cup, some of the coffee he was now drinking. He immediately dismissed the thought as ridiculous. He felt anxious telling the analyst about it. "There" and "then" the urge seemed interesting; "here" and "now," it seemed ridiculous, and in the telling made him anxious. He tells then of "other" matters, "drones about details," "laces his comments with witticisms," and says at last that he feels "warm and safe and sleepy" and feels "no pressure." The analyst now invites the patient to redirect his attention to his opening fantasy. The effort is not conspicuously successful.

We can easily say from afar that the timing *seems* a little off: that it might have been better if the analyst had waited a trifle longer, or perhaps had helped his patient to express and to explore the grounds of his anxiety, or had invited attention to one or another of the ways of managing his anxiety that the patient has just now employed, or had done one of a number of other things we do when we do what we call "working from the surface."

Some might favor, on the average, what they regard a deeper interpretation of one sort or another. Some might have searched for a comment that would be experienced as more "holding," "empathic," "supportive," "challenging," "clarifying," or something else.

Surely, though, none of us believes that it is always best to work one way or another or always to apply even our most prized rules of thumb. What I want to consider is not what else might have been done, but something about the nature of what was done. It seems to me that, in tone and timing, the analyst may have said something like this: "Listen, my dear fellow, my patience is wearing thin. Do you suppose you could stop beating around the bush and get back to your fantasy about the cup of coffee?" I am caricaturing, of course. But let's say a touch of such pressure seems present. To that degree, the analyst has here departed from his analyzing ideal to analyze the workings of the patient's mind and to avoid pushing in favor of or against particular workings. And if this is the case, here, as in the prohibition of marijuana and other drugs, the intervention appears, in form and force, to meet and to invite the very same tensions between submission and opposition that the analyst is here hoping to analyze.

Dr. Spruiell, of course, has already told that he was aware— or soon became aware—of a reciprocity of his patient's reactions and his own. "In truth," he says, "I felt a sense of *lassitude* myself, some puzzlement, and an *unwillingness*, disguised by a sense of inability, to grapple more with the issues." What a beautiful description, and how well it fits both the patient's and the analyst's salient experiences.

I do not know exactly when each aspect came to Dr. Spruiell's awareness. I would hazard the guess that from the start of the hour when he wrote down the word "cup," he was already struggling, at least at the edge of awareness, with the question of whether his "startled" response was a piece of that ideal "surprise" that alerts us to a fresh finding, or a piece, of something potentially more obstructive. I suspect, too, that throughout the hour his departures from his analyzing ideal were already beginning to alert him to those tensions of patient and self soon to be identified in the fashion Dr. Spruiell has described.

As we have seen, the saga of Ganymede and Jove, slowly and ingeniously told to himself by Dr. Spruiell and slowly and ingeniously both ignored and heard, helped him to identify the tensions represented in the tale of the almost proffered cup and in the tale of the childhood kiss of the detested daddy— tensions, at the very least between, "O leave a Kiss within the Cup," and "Beware of Greeks bearing Gifts."

Consider, please, one more hour (the hour following the hour of the cup):

The patient tells of having had more sleep, of not feeling so tired, and then says that a lot has been going on in his mind. He has realized, he says, that if his graduate students were to him as he was to his analyst, it would be *safer* to keep out of their way. This may be an insight. It seems also fair warning to his analyst to keep out of the patient's way.

He goes on to tell of his wish to *damage* the analyst. He thinks then of a woman, Boots, who uses "speed." (The analyst recalls, silently, the patient's recent fantasy of her cutting off his penis.) The patient now thinks of wanting again to use "speed."

The analyst replies: "To wake up."

I hope Dr. Spruiell will not take it amiss if I say that to me the remark seems somewhat speedy. The patient has just told of his dangerous urge to do what the analyst has absolutely forbidden. The analyst asks him to consider his motives. But what of his immediate concern of the terrifying consequences of doing, or merely wanting to do, the forbidden?

The patient then, as if wanting to make it clearer that he is not now prepared to examine his motives, says that "confessing" that he wanted to use "speed" seemed to make his "mind go blank."

The analyst presses on. He connects the urge the patient is now reluctant to explore with the one he yesterday was reluctant to explore: "It reminds me," he says, "of your thinking about bringing me coffee yesterday."

After another exchange, the patient now interrupts the analyst and asserts that when he was "confessing" about drugs the analyst interrupted him. Or to put it more precisely, the patient says: "You cut me down. *Goddamn it*, you interrupt. If I was confessing, it would *have* to mean I thought you didn't like it." He then waffles a trifle but recovers a head of steam and announces in exasperation that the analyst is "nothing but a picture on the wall."

The analyst says, "What did I do for you to react that way?"

The words may seem exploratory, but the music is not. As Dr. Spruiell tells us: "That night, I thought the question meant, unconsciously, 'I didn't do anything. Go back to sleep!' " (That night, that is, Dr. Spruiell again recognizes a departure from his analyzing ideal.)

But the patient does not go back to sleep. Through his own persistence and that of his analyst, in the context of the patient's and the analyst's joint efforts to advance the analysis and to impede, the patient now moves to that wonderful moment when Ganymede bravely and forthrightly tells Zeus that he is a "Goddamn tin God." The analyst seems to quibble a bit about the meaning of "tin." But the work goes on. And on. And through it all, the analyst sees more about himself and, in the seeing, more about his patient; and seeing more about his patient, he sees more about himself. And on. And on.

How, then, shall we regard all this? Have we simply been devoting our attention to an analyst in trouble with a troublesome patient? Perhaps. But what analyst in what analysis is not in trouble? And what patient is not troublesome? (And what patient is not in trouble, and what analyst not troublesome?)

Lacking a more complete and satisfactory view, let me put it like this:

It seems that whatever our theoretical models and methods, whatever our analyzing ideals, whatever their, and our, virtues and defects, we all depart often, in our actual work, from our models, our average methods, and our ideal of relatively nonintrusive exploration (or whatever other ideal we may care to define). But I want to go further. I want to suggest that not only do we depart *often* from our analyzing ideals—however defined—but in many ways (sometimes almost imperceptible) we *always* depart. I find it useful to regard the state of non-intrusive exploration (and other analyzing ideals) not as a steady state from which we sometimes depart, but as an elusive state we sometimes, and in some ways, approach.

When things go well, our failures to reach that state—our everyday failures—stir in us, as Dr. Spruiell has illustrated, a process of self-inquiry.[1] Those inquiries help us here and there to come a little closer to our analyzing ideals. Through mainly edge-of-awareness inquiry during analytic hours, and both edge and center inquiry after hours, we learn much about both ourselves and our patients. Our failures to reach the state we

---

[1] I use the term self-inquiry not because I love that term more, but because I love the term self-analysis less. Since the two activities, however similar in some respects, seem to me more different than alike, and since each accomplishes some ends the other cannot, I prefer not to call both by the name analysis.

seek, and our efforts to inquire into their nature, help us, therefore, to explore old tensions and new in ourselves and in our patients, and between the one and the other. And sometimes, as in this case, we are also helped to integrate theoretical matters we had previously held apart (oedipal and narcissistic, etc.).

I do not, then, regard these inquiries as merely a necessary way to avoid or decrease trouble. Self-inquiry into our persistent and inevitable failures of attitude and act seems to me a pivotal and constant feature of how we work when we work best: a critical piece of our floating attention during and after analytic hours.

I do not propose to try now to explore that range of departures from the ideal that we might call reasonable and that range we might call wild. But I do want to say that I regard these departures—when kept as small as we can manage by persistent inquiry—a useful and necessary component in the advance of every analysis. To put the matter more cautiously, many of these departures serve both to advance and to retard our work. Nevertheless, whether or not our departures are inevitable and sometimes useful, we do, I believe, when we work best, explore our mixed motives for, and the mixed consequences of, our departures. Which is to say, we work best when, having set our impossible requirements for ourselves, we train and try as hard as we can to fill them; we observe and inquire persistently into our ways and motives for failing; and from the understanding we gain, thereby, of ourselves and our patients, we manage to reach a few ends we could not otherwise reach. What a curious way we work!

This aspect of our work—the persistent failure and inquiry—is often ignored, taken for granted, or admitted grudgingly. I suspect that a more frequent, more thorough, and more joyful exploration of our inevitable departures from our analyzing ideals—especially, perhaps, of our almost imperceptible daily departures—and a more frequent sharing of our ways of inquiring into these matters, would be of considerable advantage to our methods and theories. I want to thank Dr. Spruiell for his splendid contribution to such efforts. I want to thank him, too, for his demonstration of the elaborate weave of the joint explorations of a patient and an analyst. He shows what we so often fail (and fear) to show: the struggle and the growth each analysis asks of, and makes possible for, both the patient and the analyst. He brings us, therefore, the analytical ensemble.

Dr. Spruiell has said that the quotidian of being an analyst is part of him. I like that. Since quotidian is not an everyday word, I checked my dictionary to confirm my understanding. My dictionary said that a quotidian is anything that recurs every day, especially a fever. I think Dr. Spruiell is right: the work of an analyst is a daily occupation and a fever. The fever is of mixed origin: disorder and creativity.

AFTERTHOUGHTS

Dr. Spruiell's (1984) paper and my discussion (Gardner, 1984c) were presented at a meeting of the International Psychoanalytic Association in Madrid in 1983.

A few observations about the form of this discussion:

By 1983, in several writings, I was shifting increasingly between more linear and more irregular routes of exposition. If at the time I had been asked about these and other formal oddities, I would probably have offered a double rationale: 1) the general rationale that some matters are better gotten at one way and some, another, and 2) the specific rationale that I was trying by these shifts to echo the shifts (the mind in motion?) typical of the "analyst's angle of vision" (the title of this conference) and of other would-be creative efforts.

But that would suggest a fuller conscious choice than I believe was the case. I did not decide how I wanted to write and then write. I wrote and then decided this was the way I wanted—or had—to write. If I had a choice today, I would not write this way. I once told a friend that I wished I could write with the simplicity of E. B. White. To which my friend replied, "Yes. But you are not writing *Charlotte's Web.*" I realize he was trying to be kind. I also realize that no matter how hard I tried I could not write *Charlotte's Web*. Still, I have clung to the fragment of truth in what my friend said. Though I did not realize it when I wrote my discussion of Spruiell's paper, I have since found that in writing an essay or in composing a talk about most of what I want most to write or talk about, my thoughts seem, as they did in that paper, to come most freely, and I believe usually most usefully, when they come in the form of many shifts, sometimes abrupt, back and forth between the more linear and the less. And I have found that, when I try to translate these unruly forays into more scholarly forms, much is lost in the translation. By the same token, I often have found it necessary to proceed the other way 'round. When I'm not in the right mood for writing, my thoughts often come first in more scholarly form and I'm forced then to rewrite till they become more satisfactorily irregular. I think one reason I have felt compelled to write in this completely un-E. B. White-ish way is that I cannot find words, either in scholarly or other language, adequate to address the fluidities I want most to address; therefore I must rely heavily on certain fluidities of form. Other reasons for this writerly selection (or compulsion) I leave to the imagination of anyone who likes to ruminate on the designs behind such designs.

Whatever the origins and subsequent unfoldings, I have found that one advantage of this way of proceeding is that it makes it a trifle easier to discover the hidden questions that have been shaping the piece in progress. In preparing my discussion of Spruiell's paper, for example, I discovered I had been struggling with several hidden questions about how, in addressing his clinical account, we members of the audience might clarify our similarities and differences without promoting a promiscuous pluralism, a premature ecumenicalism, or an unproductive antagonism. I then went back over what I had written and tried to bring the writing more into harmony with the intentions in those questions. I believe that my later London talk ("Is That a Fact?" see chapter 10) and other efforts, including *On Trying to Teach* (Gardner, 1994) have reflected related preoccupations and questions.

On the occasion of Spruiell's paper, my urge to find both common ground and a friendly delineation of differences was accentuated, I believe, by what I took to be signs of a brewing anti-Americanism in some sections of the international psycho-analytic community. That brew seemed often to find expression in the suggestion – implied but rarely stated flat out – that American analysts characteristically apply their visions of ego psychology so mechanically as to render psychoanalysis no longer psychoanalysis. I was pleased, therefore, to have Spruiell offer evidence that although American, and not entirely unfamiliar with ego psychology, he was also what might generally be regarded as a "real" analyst. I was also pleased – and it seemed to make him all the more real – that he elected to depart from the widely honored tradition of presenting one's work on such august occasions as if it proceeded entirely free of the impact of one's idiosyncrasies. Hence, my opening comments abut Spruiell's bravery. I believe it was also these circumstances that stirred me to refer to, and in postdiscussion discussions to make more explicit, my growing conviction that it is not as useful to color the analyst colorless as to proceed on the assumption that our idiosyncrasies influence for good and for bad all that we do and the corollary assumption that without persistent self-analysis – I had begun to prefer calling it self-inquiry – there is no such thing as psychoanalysis.

Chapter Four

===========

AFTER?

After the hours? After which hours? After all the hours of an analysis? After each hour of an ongoing analysis? After the hours for whom? After the hours for the patient? Or after the hours for the analyst?

I want to look at a small piece of all that: the after-the-hour experiences of the analyst, which is to say, my after-the-hour experiences when analyzing a patient, which is also to say the after-the-hours of my own analysis, now continued in my self-inquiries after my patient's and my hours together.

I assume that the distinction between after the hour and during may be useful for some ends—a useful fiction—but it can blur our vision for ways in which after the hour is part of the hour: part of the hour before and part of the hour after. Every hour is surely a before, and every before is surely an after. That is my subject, and I shall try to examine it by examining myself.

Some years ago, while trying to observe what happens to an

analyst during analytic hours, I found myself trying to observe what happens to an analyst after the hours. I noticed in particular that while my patient and I were parting, and for ten seconds or so after, I seemed to remain in a state of floating attention rather like the one I hope to be in during the hour. I remain in that state, that is, if I do not disrupt it by turning too quickly to "practical" matters.

In those few seconds after the hour, and occasionally for considerably longer, in a curious way that I cannot sufficiently explain, nor even sufficiently describe, I feel myself still to be "in touch" with my patient. In those moments, my floating attention seems to continue, along with, in my imagination, the play of my floating attention with my patient's free association.

I am, then, more than ordinarily apt to see, and to be aware of seeing, visual images. They are brief. They persist for only a few tenths of a second. Having become aware of these images, I have become accustomed, when time and other considerations permit, to associate to their elements as patients and analysts sometimes do in their first steps toward the analysis of a dream.

I have described these efforts elsewhere (Gardner, 1989). I want to sum up what I found and go on from there. When I pursue far enough my associations to my visual images, they reveal, in each instance with each patient, rich likenesses in the conflicts, character, and circumstances, past and present, of my patient and myself, and in the tensions then at work between us.

Recovering and exploring such images soon became a steady part of my work. And though at first I saw all this mainly as an effort to explore visual thinking, I realized gradually and increasingly that these after-the-hour inquiries were changing how I saw my patient and how I saw myself.

I found that I had been doing much I had not known I was doing. I found that my images reflected not only many of my conflicts and defects, but many of my edge-of-awareness attempts to inquire into these and into other tensions and dilemmas. I found that each of my images reflected edge-of-awareness inquiries I had been pursuing during the hour and for several days or weeks before. And I found that each image reflected edge-of-awareness inquiries my patient had been pursuing during the hour and for several days or weeks before. It seemed to me, that is, that at edge of awareness my patient and I had each been advancing and obstructing similar inquiries and that the advancing and the obstructing of the one was shaping and shaped by the advancing and the obstructing of the other.

I could, therefore, no longer persist in my earlier view that I was simply "resonating" to my patient. More and more it seemed clear that what I was doing—and right along had been doing—was selecting, matching, and advancing from the on-going edge-of-awareness inquiries of my patient and myself agendas important to each. It seemed to me, that is, that this selecting, matching, and advancing was an unending activity in and between my patient and myself.

Little by little, I formed the opinion that I was both pursuing an idiosyncratic interest in my visual images and trying to catch a glimpse of a common and constant thrust in the play of my patient's free association and my floating attention: the advancing of almost but not quite recognized inquiries essential to the well-being and the growth of both my patient and myself. (I found these to be inquiries mainly into large and never fully solvable problems of mutuality: dilemmas and choices we usually call "surface," which, if explored, lead farther and farther into what we usually call "depths.")

When, through these after-the-hour efforts, I had become more aware of those mutualities of inquiry, I found that I was expanding my floating attention, during the hours, to include more and more of my patient's edge-of-awareness inquiries and his or her ways of advancing and obstructing them. This led me, in turn, after the hours, to notice more of my own, and on and on in reciprocal exchange.

But what does it mean to "expand" floating attention? I do not mean that I set out directly to do this. One does not, of course, directly narrow or expand floating attention. Nor did I remark directly on my patient's inquiries or my own; I doubt I'd have been able even if I'd wanted. My awareness was rarely so clear as that. Rather, I relied on my after-the-hour activities to shape "spontaneously" my during-the-hour attitudes and acts. I did not supervise or instruct myself to do this or do that.

Sometimes, I could see, looking back, how what I did after one hour had affected what I had seen or said in the next. More often, I merely had a general impression that by pursuing my after-the-hour inquiries more vigorously, or, at least, more openly, I was able to sense more clearly the directions and convolutions of my patient's inquiry and my own. It seemed to me, too, that both the timing and the tone of my remarks were better whenever, by new inquiry and discovery, I managed to see that what I was trying to understand was not only my patient but myself.

I was pleased and I was challenged. I was determined no longer to confine my after-the-hour inquiries to those times when I regarded myself in trouble; rather, I regarded myself in trouble whenever I failed to inquire.

Whether my enthusiastic assessment was correct is another question. It's always hard to know if changes of method are merely a private accommodation to personal needs and, if so, whether a good accommodation or poor. But good or poor, I soon found the method I had chosen—or perhaps had no choice but to choose—was not an unmitigated blessing. It was slow going, arduous, and demanding of time and energy.

And having committed myself to after-hour inquiries of the sort I have outlined, I was distressed to find that I could only occasionally do what I had hoped. After hours, I sometimes saw no images. And when I saw images, my efforts to associate to or make sense of them were often unsuccessful. Finally, having more trouble than usual in recovering and exploring my images, I realized I had, in compensation, been pursuing other after-the-hour inquiries. Here is an instance.

One evening I sat down to write notes about an analytic hour. As I reached for my pen, however, I recalled a moment of the hour with the next patient that same day. I recalled that at the outset of that next hour I had suddenly experienced a misgiving that I had lost my pen and had then quickly searched for it till I came upon the pen in the very same shirt pocket in which I usually put it and in which, without giving the matter much thought, I usually know it to be.

On considering the event, I was struck first by the compelling nature of my need. Since I do not make notes during analytic hours and so had no apparent need for a pen, and since there was therefore not even a flimsy rationalization possible for my behavior, I was struck by my during-the-hour failure to notice anything peculiar or to wonder about the relation of my pen search to the ongoing events of the analysis.

From the form of this incident and the overtones of even this sparse account—an account taken from the notes I made that evening—you will have no difficulty inferring some aspects of the anxiety I was facing. As I thought that evening about the relation of that anxiety to my compelling search, it seemed clear to me that my ritual must have served not only to shift the locus of my anxiety from below to above, and from the more intense concern to the less, but also, through its happy conclusion, to reassure me that what I feared missing was not missing at all, but exactly where it ought to be.

As I thought more about my anxiety and about the examination followed by relief, I was reminded of Freud's observations about the reassuring purpose of dreams in which the dreamer fears failing an examination that in waking life the dreamer has already passed. I wondered, then, whether, like dreamers of such dreams, I had secretly anticipated some sort of ordeal and had reassured myself in advance that all would be, as I had just found in regard to my pen, all right. ("You need not worry; you see how unfounded your fears prove.")

My attention—still in the evening after the hour—then shifted from the moment in question to the manner in which my thoughts had now unfolded. It struck me that in thinking of my need to reassure myself I had now repeated something of the same. It seemed to me, that is, that even if my thoughts of the examination dreams might be apt, I was trying, by referring to Freud, to reassure myself that he, who was talking of his own examination dreams, had acted in the same way I had acted in the moment in question.

That I seemed to be stretching logic by comparing my behavior awake with his in a dream seemed not to trouble me at all. But I did begin to wonder then if Freud had actually said that he had experienced such dreams. I turned to his *Interpretation of Dreams* and, of course, found that he had. How odd. I realized that, again, in thinking about the incident of the pen, I seemed to have repeated a part. I had constructed a concern, an examination, and a reassurance.

I saw that in my after-the-hour drift, I had somehow recreated—or been pulled back into—the music of that during-the-hour incident: I had searched for something I seemed to have lost or forgotten, only to find it exactly where I'd hoped and known it—without being sure I knew it—to be. Thinking then of this prestidigitation, I was reminded of the demonstration of magic in Mark Twain's *A Connecticut Yankee in King Arthur's Court:* the protagonist, having traveled back in time, predicts to the awed populace the coming of an eclipse of the sun, an event that is part of his own past and whose occurrence he has predicted by looking up the facts in his almanac.

I also remembered, then, a moment in my childhood when my father's knowledge of the written word (the pen again?) had made him seem a magician. As I looked next at the flow of my associations, the earlier and the later, it seemed to me that I'd been trying repeatedly to reassure myself that I possessed both ordinary things and abilities and wondrous things and abilities, and that I was consequently to be ranked with my father and Freud, great predictors of things past, and of the Connecticut Yankee, great predictor, no matter how questionable, of things to come. I was struck, too, by my tangential preoccupation with the question of who really had what and who was only pretending to have what he had not.

I do not suggest that these are the only interpretations possible or that they could not have been made through swifter or more convincing means. But these were the associations and interpretations possible – and impossible – to me at that particular time. And these were the particular and circuitous routes of the after-the-hour inquiry I needed then to travel. As I look back now, those routes seem to me remarkably tangential and to miss more than they cover. But that is always the case. The other person's route of inquiry and one's own viewed from afar always seem to wander all over; only one's own ongoing inquiry, viewed by oneself close up, seems to go straight to the mark. I want to mention this matter of routes of inquiry now and come back to it later.

My attention next turned, somewhat belatedly it seems to me now looking back, to the question of what I might have been anticipating at the outset of the hour and why I needed to address it so importunately in the search for my pen. Aided by the work I had just done and the feelings stirred, I recalled that the first of the two patients, in an hour I regarded particularly fruitful, had made a remark I now recognized as characteristic. She had said on the edge between open criticism of herself and covert criticism of me, "Well, I wasn't able to get very far today."

This does not sound strikingly critical. At the time I was unaware of reacting to it at all. But on further consideration that evening I realized that in the play between my patient's free associations and my floating attention, I had felt a cutting edge; and my pen search with the next patient was an extended consequence. That is, I gathered that similarities in what was then emerging in the analyses of both patients had led me to try to recover from the first hour – "after the hour" – in the second and by the same device to protect myself from expected attack in the second.

I then recalled that the second patient had begun by saying she felt "anxious." Threatening? Looking back, I saw what I must have sensed but failed to recognize: she had spoken in a way she often did when she meant not to explore but rather to complain that her analysis and I had been failing to help her. I saw that she did intend to explore, though hesitantly, how I might respond to her voicing, or almost voicing, a criticism of me. Which apparently was why, responding to the slight barb at the end of one patient's hour, I had responded to a slight and similar barb at the outset of the hour with the next patient by searching for my pen.

In the second hour, one thing then led to another till, after a question and a comment or two from me, my patient attributed her anxiety to an increase in her competence to "speak up." She said that she feared that, by advancing in these ways and by meeting men on equal footing rather than deferring, she would threaten them, stir their anger, and provoke attacks. A few months later she said she now felt anxious and had the urge to run. When I highlighted her associative drift, she recalled what she had "forgot": she had thought "angrily" a moment before that I was about to "announce angrily" that she envied men and was "cutting" toward them and that it was only because of her own anger that she feared the anger of men.

On reconsidering all this after the hour, and on adding my reflections regarding my pen search, I began to see several ways that my patient often timidly voiced her resentments and in turn became more timid and resentful. And I began to see that in dealing with the belligerence of men in reaction to her competence, whether a belligerence she had evoked or not, she was so plagued by her hidden intentions, resentments, and vaguely perceived but not quite acknowledged "cuts" that she was never sure who had done what to whom.

I began also to see that I had been threatened by some of my patient's fantasies and acts and by some of her growing abilities to "speak up." And I realized that several times *before* the incident of the pen, I had reached for my pen in another sense. I had become too wordy. Moreover, in trying to prove the pen mightier than the sword, I had become a bit belligerent in the very way she had feared, expected, and, as I later learned, observed.

Musing more, I realized that some aspects of my anxiety and my responses to it—subtle attacks with words on the feared attacker—resembled some of the ways of my patient. And, seeing this, I saw that although I do not usually play lost and found as I had in the incident of the pen, I had here also done something characteristic of my patient. I realized, that is, that she had shown an extensive and persistent propensity to forget words, to search for them irritably, and then delightedly to find them. And I then realized that this was but one piece of a larger tendency to lose and then regain other verbal and mental faculties, and to lose and regain physical possessions, or, failing that, to replace them quickly, thereby proving whenever she could that whatever is missing matters not.

My attention then shifted again to myself. I was struck that the question of what I had lost and what I had not, no matter how narrowly based a question in its depths and how mechanically answered in my pen search, was a question of considerably broader scope than I had at first grasped. I realized that this question was one piece of a long sequence of questions, some hidden, some not, that I had been pursuing persistently for several weeks or more.

It's hard to put such clusters of questions into words. And they become different once put. I inferred, however, that these particular questions came and went something like this:

Now, in one context and now in another, I had been almost but not quite aware of asking how I might attain a fuller economy of means. In analyzing, in painting, in writing (another allusion of the pen, I suppose), and in other of my affairs, I seemed (in retrospect) to have been struggling over and over with questions of how to achieve more through less. And in trying to set aside old ways for new, I seemed to have been inquiring repeatedly into the consequences, trying, that is, to assess repeatedly what I had gained and what I had lost, and what others might judge to be the gains and the losses. In these and other respects, the incident of the pen, followed one way, led to my underworld, and, followed another, led to links between underworld and currently experienced outer. Which I suppose goes to show how deep is the surface.

Following these findings, the world in question turned into the other of my underworlds. "Economy of means" called back suddenly the words of a song of the thirties, "It Ain't Necessarily So," which I happened to favor in boyhood:

Little David was small but oh my!
Little David was small but oh my!
He fought big Goliath who lay down and dieth!
Little David was small but oh my!

And another stanza, as if to make matters clearer, tells that the "old man" — now given another name — is less able than he seems:

Methus'lah lived nine hundred years,
Methus'lah lived nine hundred years,
But who calls dat livin' when no gal'll give in
To no man what's nine hundred years?
    [From *Porgy and Bess*, George and Ira Gershwin]

"After-the-hour" drifts such as the one that followed the incident of the pen take much time to tell. But, though the telling is slow and tortured, (quite lacking in "economy of means"), the originals move quickly, I find, if they move at all.

L et's retrace our steps. Having found myself sometimes unable to live up to my ideal of exploring my visual images, I began pursuing other, though related, after-the-hour inquiries, inquiries into departures from other ideals of my analyzing attitudes and acts. I am not referring to gross departures. I had long been accustomed to inquiring into those. I am referring to slight slackenings of attention, slight delays or rushes of my responses, and slight shifts in their intensity or tone, and other shifts of attention, feeling, urge, intervention or other activity so brief or low key as to be easily overlooked.

As in the case of the incident of the pen, these after-the-hour inquiries have often seemed not merely a remote review of in-hour events, but a re-creation, and beyond that a magnification, of the in-hour. Though sometimes these after-the-hour inquiries helped me to explore in smaller doses what in-hour had been too intense, more often they seemed to heighten or dramatize, and therefore make easier to explore, what earlier had been invisible or, if visible, seemingly insignificant.

When these after-the-hour inquiries were at all successful, they usually revealed much about myself and much about my patient. And as my visual images had done, and often continued to do, these inquiries into what I hoped to be mini-departures from my analyzing ideals, led over and over to tensions then at work between my patient and me.

Consultations with colleagues about their analytical work have heightened my suspicion and my hope that I am not alone in these departures and tensions; rather that the complementarities of preoccupation and reaction of my patients and me reflect the highly evocative two-way effects of the ordinary play of a patient's free associations and an analyst's floating attention, aided a bit by the amplifying effects of persistent after-the-hour inquiries. In putting the matter so, I do not mean to minimize the range of my own psychopathology of everyday life or the frailties of my analytical work. I mean to testify to what have seemed to me the benefits of after-the-hour efforts to inquire into the specifics of that pathology and those frailties. I mean also to highlight the possibility of an inevitability that the nature of the analytical situation has the repeated effect of pulling the patient and the analyst a bit, or a lot, away from whatever stance the analyst regards an ideal. I suspect this holds true whatever the ideals, theory, interests, and character of the analyst may be. And I suspect that when things go relatively well, these departures, remaining relatively slight, induce in the analyst one or another form of the during- and after-the-hour inquiry that leads not only to corrections in approach but also to a fuller understanding of self and other and, sometimes, to changes in method and theory. All this, I believe, is a ubiquitous, usually automatic, and often imperceptible piece of the analyst's work.

What I have tried to describe are efforts to bring to the center of awareness some of what we ordinarily do at the edge. And, although in stressing center I do not mean to slight edge, I have found these self-conscious, after-the-hour inquiries of unexpected advantage not only in taking a sounding of what is salient between my patient and me, but in making my floating attention during hours float freer. I think it helps also in my approach to my patient when I can at least occasionally see clearly that all that goes poorly is not my patient's doing, and all that goes well, not my own.

Moreover, having found freshly (the freshly is surprisingly necessary) that it is easier to grasp some things after the hour and some during, some with my patient and some when alone, some in one mood and some in another, and some when thinking one way and some when thinking another, it seems then to happen that when I find something in the one circumstance that I had missed in the other, the finding is more a matter for enjoyment and less for chagrin. Feeling so, I find it easier to try to discover how it is that what I see now I could not see before.

But why do my visual images and my departures from my analytical ideals prove such elaborate reflections of both my hour inquiry? I find nothing of comparable value for the pursuit of self-inquiry except perhaps my dreams. The answer may lie in that fact. These episodes, though not entirely dreams, are dreamlike. And these episodes, though partly my constructions, are not my constructions alone. They are in some respects the joint dreamlike productions of my patients' efforts and my own. And, being dreamlike, they have the advantage after the hour of evoking in me a drift very like the ones in which they were first fashioned. And though not full-fledged dreams, they are, like dreams, highly evocative and, being compounded of similar forces and devices, often prove similarly rewarding for exploration minutes after, hours after, days after, weeks after, months after, and years after. Accordingly, when things go relatively well, after-the-hour inquiries advance in-hour inquiries and in-hour inquiries advance after-the-hour. And, in these circumstances, after-the-hour inquiries and in-hour seem almost, though not quite, indivisible.

AFTERTHOUGHTS

"After?" was written in 1984 in response to an invitation from *Etudes Freudienne* to set down a few ideas on the topic: "After the Hours" (Gardner, 1984a). I took this to be an inkblotian invitation to respondents to proceed as we saw fit. Others seem to have taken it in the same spirit.

I tried to pursue notions I had touched upon in discussing Spruiell's paper in Madrid, in *Self Inquiry* and in Paris meetings with a group of French and American colleagues optimistically designated as a Franco-American alliance. In one way or another, I was at that time preoccupied with the unsteady and sometimes hazardous transition (the hazards were soon to become a bit clearer) from viewing psychoanalysis as a one-party enterprise to viewing it (sometimes) as a two-. To that end, I tried to glimpse and set down in "After?" an instance of an after-the-hour re-creation of an in-hour angle of vision. I tried, that is, to glimpse and set down a fragment of an instance of a double vision. That was my conscious intent: to tell something of my analyzing experience and to illustrate a habit of observation that might offer a small window into the elaborate play between in-hour and after-the-hour analytic experience and, in that frame, the play between patient and analyst.

I began to muse then, and since have mused more, about the curious circumstance that after, a century of experience with the free association method and with the requisite "evenly hovering attention," we know surprisingly little about the workings of that method and that attention. And it began to seem then, and now seems to me more persistently, that we were and still are missing an opportunity to learn a bit more about the nature of our own and our patients' contributions to our joint explorations.

In retrospect, however, it seems to me that in trying to observe these matters I was also pursuing a cluster of almost but not quite recognized epistemological questions. If I had recognized them then, I might have said I had become increasingly preoccupied with trying to pursue questions about how it comes about that what we perceive – whether of "inner" worlds or "outer" – is always a happening seen *in* a looking glass or, at best, a happening seen *through* a looking glass. On second thought, I might find those mirror images too static. I might say instead that I was preoccupied with the "relational" nature of our perceptions (Rosenfield, 1993), whether perceptions of what we experience as something in the "outer" world before us, or as part of our "inner" world of memories, sensations, affects, phantasies, or anything else. Or, playing leapfrog with the philosopher Thomas Nagel, I might say today that I was pursuing questions in "After?" about how it comes about that every "fact" is a partial and evolving view from a partial and evolving somewhere by a partial and evolving somebody.

Chapter Five

TO BE (OR NOT TO BE)
AN ANALYST

I am assuming that someone might be wondering, or some day might wonder, whether to become an analyst and if so, where to begin. To that someone, I want to say briefly what I think it means to be an analyst and what I think an institute should and should not be.

To be an analyst, it seems to me, is to be where the so-called two worlds—the *humanistic* and the *scientific*—are most clearly one.

To be an analyst is to be where the pursuit of one's everyday tasks—everyday, but rarely routine—*affirms and reaffirms the worth of the individual and the worth of the life considered.*

I regard these as wonderful places to be.

To be an analyst is to live, elaborately and intensely, many lives. To be an analyst is to experience the strange and the foreign and to find ways in which they are neither so strange nor so foreign.

To be an analyst is to help others to advance their struggles to know themselves by advancing one's own struggles, and to advance one's own by helping others to advance theirs. That seems to me also not too shabby a place to be.

To be an analyst is to see and experience closeup the ubiquity, the power, the tragedy, and the grandeur of our amazingly conflicting intentions.

To be an analyst is to have the chance to find unities between analysis and most other interests one might have or develop and, in the doing, to enrich the one and the other. To be an analyst is to be in a field in which the borders between vocation and avocation are beautifully shadowed.

To be an analyst, as Kenneth Clark said of being engaged in the building of other Gothic structures, is to be engaged in *serious play*.

To gain such increases in space for the imagination, you will have to sit stiller and stick tighter to a schedule than any sensible person would choose; and you will have to invest much energy and time to earn the privilege of sitting there. If you are a psychiatrist, the financial rewards will be less than you could earn by practicing general psychiatry and much less than you could earn in other enterprises for which you may have the skills. Nevertheless, if from one point of view you may be a low paid medic, you will, from another, be a highly paid academic.

At any rate, the fascination of being an analyst is sufficient so that some of us feel it's not a bad way to go. In fact, I think I can safely say that being an analyst is the sort of thing you will love, if you love that sort of thing. You understand that it is not my aim to persuade anyone to pursue such a peculiar commitment, only briefly to describe it.

Assuming that you do make the decision—on some grounds or other—to pursue such a calling, at which institute should you seek to begin? I would advise you, if you were to ask, to seek institutes with some characteristics and to eschew institutes with others. I would advise you to seek an institute where candidates and teachers have a concern for people, an itch for learning, a craving for adventure, an addiction to exploration, and a passion for psychoanalysis.

If you want to learn to play the piano, seek the help of those who *play* the piano, who play a lot of piano, and who love to play the piano. Beware of those teachers and students whose hearts are committed elsewhere and who are merely keeping a hand in the playing of the piano. Which is to say, beware of those who regard psychoanalysis mainly as a stepping stone to academic, political, or other ends. You know how to recognize them. You've seen more than enough wherever you have been.

I would advise you to seek a school where the teachers and students treat each other and themselves with respect. Beware of schools where wheeling and dealing, one-up-manship, and empire building are the order of the day.

Seek a school where the atmosphere is unhurried and contemplative. Beware of schools where education is confused with manufacture, schools where the attitudes, acts, and advertising are more reminiscent of commerce than of a school for post-post-postgraduate education. Beware of schools where the concern is so much with living up to minimal standards that everyone happily does.

Seek a school where the candidates and teachers love the rhythms and complexities of learning and teaching. Seek a school where teachers and students love to teach and to learn, expect to teach and to be taught by each other, and expect to teach and be taught by themselves. Beware of schools with teachers and students who are content to dispense and swallow "the word." Beware of teachers and students who refuse to reveal and to explore what they know and what they do not know. Beware of schools where the pursuit of knowledge takes a back seat to the pursuit of status.

Seek a school where the teachers and students try to know the school's virtues and defects and try to make that school a better place for each other. Beware of schools in which the students and teachers settle for conventional autocratic arrangements or conventional pseudo-democratic alternatives. Beware of schools where tokenism passes for an effort to advance common cause.

Seek a school administered by those who do not love administration and whose administrative skills are conspicuously stunted. Beware of schools in which the teachers and students are unabashedly expert in Robert's Rules of Order or the procedures, requirements, rules, and regulations of national and international organizations. Most especially beware of schools where eyes flash and color improves when issues of administration are considered.

Seek a school large enough for diversity, small enough for intimacy. (Schools, like everything else, have an optimum size.) Beware of schools in which size is prized above all. Beware of schools in which the increase in numbers of members, of well-wishers, or of material possessions is regarded as improvement per se, and in which energies are more and more devoted to achieving that end at the expense of others.

Seek a school where they seek to put first things first. Seek a school that seeks to be classical, not merely popular. Which is to say, seek a school that seeks the relatively timeless and is not cowed by the popularity of the modern or the antique. Seek a school, that is, that seeks old classics and new.

All this is mainly to say, I would advise you, if you were to ask me, to choose an institute with very great care. No institute can teach you what you need to know; but some can provide a climate in which you may begin to discover it.

The climate is what counts most. And to diagnose the climate of an institute will take all your talents at reading the lines and reading between the lines. If you fail to exercise those talents, and if, on the assumptions that you can't got too far wrong, you go like a lemming where your friends have gone, you may find yourself not where you had hoped, but at sea. Institutes are like everything else. The worst are dreadful; the best are barely good enough. I would advise you, therefore, if you were to ask my advice:

Seek the very best you can find.

AFTERTHOUGHTS

I have never understood why analysts insist on calling their schools "Institutes." I suppose it comes of the same impulses and the same historical twists as calling the activities in their schools "training," of calling consultants "supervisors," of calling classes "seminars," and of calling students "candidates."

Misgivings notwithstanding, on the occasion of an open house of The Psychoanalytic Institute of New England, East—generally more happily called PINE—I accepted the invitation to offer a few introductory remarks about becoming an analyst and about choosing a psychoanalytic "Institute." These remarks were made to a group of persons who had responded to an invitation to meet the faculty of PINE. The nature of that invitation made it reasonable to anticipate that a few of those persons might be considering the possibility of seeking psychoanalytic schooling. Still, that couldn't be taken for granted. Besides, I wasn't sure (nor am I now) if recruiting and psychoanalytic schooling are a good mix. For these and other reasons, I was pulled between my enthusiasm for the benefits of a psychoanalytic schooling and of becoming an analyst, and my determination not to "sell" psychoanalysis or any other noble enterprise to these young persons in the throes of deciding how they wanted to spend a large part of their lives.

In the main, this tension—to sell or not to sell—seems to have resulted in a relatively soft sell, or at least as soft a sell as I could manage. But, in retrospect, I suppose the fact that it was still unquestionably a sell was betrayed repeatedly and perhaps nowhere more clearly than in the half-serious and half-tongue-in-cheek suggestion that the pay for an analyst might be regarded low for a medic but might also be regarded high for an academic.

As I look beyond the exigencies of that moment, my choice to highlight a positive possibility in a seemingly negative situation seems a reflection of old and continuing preoccupations and questions similar to those that had led me earlier to my concluding remarks about the Hudson River (see chapter 3), similar to those that crop up in the incident of the weather "trying to clear" (chapter 6), and similar to earlier and later expressions. For all that, if I were now to try to find a silver lining in my long search for silver linings, I would say that under especially favorable circumstances that search has shaped and been shaped by struggles—largely hidden—to find useful possibilities for that silvery proclivity and ways to limit, where possible, its most fatuous and dangerous possibilities. In that respect, I suspect that one powerful appeal of the two impossible professions I have chosen to pursue—psychoanalysis and teaching—may have been located in the many opportunities these endeavors provide separately and together for addressing that challenge.

As I view my PINE open house remarks from another latter day perspective—though perhaps not entirely unrelated—they seem also to reflect a persisting preoccupation with the unities of apparently disparate worlds: those, for example, of vocations and avocations, analysts and patients, medics and academics. And that urge to find unities in apparent disparities seems also to crop up in my stress on the need for a harmony between the nature of the field to be studied and the nature of the school in which that studying is to take place: in this instance, a harmony between an exploratory stance—including habits of self-inquiry—in the psychoanalytic endeavor and an exploratory stance—including habits of self-inquiry—in a school in which attention to that endeavor is attempted.

All of which seems to have foreshadowed my increasing preoccupation with the dilemmas and challenges of teaching and learning. That preoccupation had already expressed itself, without my fully grasping it, in a collection of letters called *Cher Pierre* (Gardner, submitted), letters that purported to tell an innocent abroad how to speak French to the French when you know very little French. Those same preoccupations foreshadowed in *Cher Pierre* and in the effort not to recruit students for PINE took fuller shape a decade later in a slim volume called *On Trying To Teach* (Gardner, 1994a).

Chapter Six

=======

ON TALKING TO OURSELVES
Some Self-Analytical Reflections
on Self-Analysis

One day, a friend said of the unsettled weather, "It looks as if it's going to clear."

"Yes," I said, "but it's been *trying* all morning to clear and each time it's failed."

Hours later I was struck—though I'd not been before—that I'd talked of the weather as if the weather had a will. And having noted my animism, I said to myself, in some way or other, "I wonder who is *it* who's been trying all morning to clear?" (I say "some way or other" because private conversations go mainly in zig-zags, not reportorial lines.)

Though my question might seem to have implied the answer, I needed a few moments to catch up. One thing led to another and another—word, image, feeling—till I realized at last that all morning long I'd been "under the weather" and I'd been trying to clear my dampened spirits. Understand that, I realized an unrecognized reason for my unrecognized distress and felt a quick relief from the distress I'd not realized I was trying to relieve.

Later—several hours later—"It's been trying to clear" came back to my mind and with it an incident I'd several months earlier put in my journal and forgot. On that earlier occasion, seated before a window and looking out at the grey wintry sky, I'd been wondering, if I were to paint it, how I might catch its varied and varying tones? Though the sky at first seemed a strangely uniform *blue*-grey, one small section was slowly lightening and, almost imperceptibly, taking on, in turn, one *warmer* hue and another.

Musing about these idiosyncrasies of the sky and the problems they might present in painting, and having set down those musings in my journal, I turned to something else. I was startled, therefore, when almost a half hour later, the entire sky took a turn for the better and seemed to confer on my earlier observations the status of an unrecognized prediction of improvements to come.

I wondered then whether similar—though unrecognized—seeings of slight brightenings of the sky might have been what had made me able on other occasions unaccountably to predict the coming of sunnier weather and to do so considerably before the appearance of those favorable signs of which I was aware (changes in humidity, wind, behavior of the birds, etc.). I noted and put down these wonderings with no further comment and, till the moment at hand, no further thought.

But looking back at that earlier moment of sky gazing, looking back, that is, in the light of the current incident of the weather's "trying to clear," I realized that on both occasions I'd not, as I'd first thought, observed casually, but rather searched diligently, for those brightenings of the sky. I wondered then how widespread my habit might be of searching in this way first for gloomy skies and then for my favorite harbingers of what the English call "sunny spots."

My thoughts turned from one thing to another and then to a familiar pattern of my outlook I'd long been accustomed to call "looking for silver linings." I realized at once as I'd not realized

before that to speak of my inclination to look for silver linings
was to tell not only a metaphorical truth but a literal truth about
the conditions of the sky on which, as I'd now seen, I tended to
fasten attention. I realized, too, that such vivifying of ossified
metaphors comes always as a surprise, which includes the
surprise that the obvious should be a surprise.

In talking to oneself it seems possible—though hard to say
how—to say more than one thing at once. Or almost at once.
When I thought of the literality of my search for silver linings,
it struck me simultaneously as quite understandable that I like
to paint skyscapes, especially the contrasts between lights and
darks, and am partial to the use of watercolors, a medium so
suited to capturing the vagaries of light and to creating illusions
that a static picture is changing from one fluid state to another.

On the *darker* side, my associations took a sudden turn
toward the past and wandered back by a long path to my much
earlier years. I recalled at last, and was startled to recall, a
custom of my childhood—I could not recall being aware of it
before—a custom of tempering sadness by seeking comfort in
"Mother Nature." I remembered most vividly that in a place
well known for its gloomy weather, at a time of special reason
for my being under the weather, I'd gone off from time to time
to a secret nook, stared gloomily at the gloomy skies, and then
felt a special delight in watching the skies clear. I say I
"recalled" those moments long past, but I think it truer to say
that for an instant I "stepped back." (Or as we like to put it in
our Latinate way, I regressed.) And I recalled too, or in my
mind's eye re-viewed, a moment in the same time and space
when, sitting quietly in my private nook, I had observed
joyfully the winter suddenly give way to spring.

Proclivity becomes perception becomes memory becomes
metaphor becomes proclivity becomes perception becomes
memory and on and on and back and forth in never-ending
exchange. Which is to say, it seems safe to say, my perception
of brightening skies was no idle perception. (If there is any
such thing as an idle perception.) Looking back at my climatic
associations, I surmised that at such moments as had now
come to my attention, I first carefully blurred the distinction

between my gloom and nature's—making the sky, so to speak, a large parabolic mirror—and then cheered myself by finding a bright spot to reflect, abet, and magnify a brightening of my inner nature.

This overview—dare I say these insights?—and a rush of thoughts about the probable effects of a known challenge in my still earlier years struck me with peculiar force and, in the manner of a good-enough interpretation, or series of interpretations, impressed me as new and convincing. They stirred in me a sense of understanding and a feeling of satisfaction, and rapidly brought to my mind what I perceived to be related events, thoughts, images, and feelings, some of which, as far as I could recall, had previously been unavailable, and others, though available, had previously seemed unrelated.

For months after, I experienced fresh bursts of resonant associations that, with further exploration, enlarged my views of several times and places of my past and several current events. To put the matter another way, my *representations* of the two weather incidents have been and remain highly evocative. I believe that even now, if I were to associate anew, my associations would lead me in still other directions. I want to mention this matter of the evocative power of *particular configurations*—genres—for one person and another and come back to it later.

Of the intimacies of these weather incidents—of the oedipal, preoedipal, and postoedipal lights in the dark—I'll say no more. Public confession suffers a double difficulty: whoever confesses, faces a loss of privacy; whoever listens is made to bear uneasy witness to events whose recounting runs the all too narrow path between candor and sentimentality. (I shall add only that I believe one new spur to my long search for the light in the dark was my recently reaching the age of 60, an event made more complicated by my having moved so speedily to 60 from 16.)

What shall we call such perambulations of the mind? Self-analysis? I don't know. I don't like the term self-analysis. It seems to me to carry misleading connotations of a similarity, perhaps identity, between what we ordinarily call psychoanalysis and what we call self-analysis. I prefer to reserve the terms psychoanalysis and analysis for the special circumstances and possibilities of the two-party situation and to refer to the climate and procedures of the solo endeavor as self-inquiry, a term that, whatever its limitations, means for me something different from, and somewhere between, some aspects of psychoanalysis and ordinary introspection. But with that objection stated, and since the term is so entrenched in our literature and everyday parlance, I shall refer in these remarks to "self-analysis."

Self-analyzers, it seems, have strangely stringent requirements for gathering self-analytical materials, the kinds of materials they gather, and the ways in which, and conditions under which, they customarily proceed. What works best for each is arrived at by long trial and error. For the serious self-analyzer, these idiosyncratic necessities change again and again through more trial and error. I gather from these doings that what is called self-analysis by one person may be very different from what is called self-analysis by another. So, when we discuss self-analysis—perhaps even more than when we discuss psychoanalysis—we may be discussing approaches more different than alike.

My own self-analytical efforts begin mainly in one of three ways:

1) Often, as in the case of the clearing weather, some current event catches my attention and seems unaccountably and irresistibly to demand consideration. As a rule, through no conscious plan, I seem strongly to prefer as a starting point these conditions of the *immediate, the inadvertent, and the demanding.*

More often than not, when self-analysis begins so, I have a sense of its being "despite" myself. Which is also to say, my self-analysis seems to go better in the face of a *slight but surmountable resistance:* strong enough so I disavow active seeking but not so strong that I reject the seemingly unsolicited invitation. (I imagine that Freud, in those letters to Fliess in which he tells of ideas "dawning" upon him, or of "waiting" for ideas to come, and the like, is not indulging in romantic excess but trying to describe a similar mix of *resistance and receptivity*.)

2) For more systematic efforts at self-analysis, I've found it handy to keep a journal where I set down from time to time, daily when I can manage, whatever is most vividly on my mind or, as it sometimes seems, whatever is hardest to get off my mind. Whether that takes the form of an image, a word, a phrase, or a full-blown essay, it seems most often to begin with, and frequently to return to, something I've seen, actually seen or visualized. Most often in the writing, when things go best, I have the curious illusion that what I'm writing has nothing whatever to do with me but refers only to some "external event" that has inescapably caught my eye. (In the midst, therefore, of the *activity* of "keeping" a journal is the *passivity* of a *conscious surrender of choice of subject*: an intercourse, so to speak, between the more active and the more passive.) It's one thing to know abstractly that all I write has much to do with me, it's another to know it in the act of writing. When things go best, I don't at first know that what I write, and how I write is about me—indeed, *is* me. At least, I manage for a while not to know that I know it.

I find it necessary, or at least favorable, for my self-analysis not to regard particular materials, whether dreams or anything else, as something I "should" or "must" explore. I know that some self-analyzers find it routinely fruitful to analyze their dreams or something else. I do not. Rather, I stick strictly to the policy of exploring whatever grips me, whatever form it takes and no matter how trivial or promising it may at first seem. I've learned that if, in advance, I tip off my resistances and other self-analytical saboteurs that I plan automatically and routinely to analyze my dreams or anything else, they pile up so many obstacles to self-analysis—a pastime sorely limited at best—that I discover little or nothing I did not know before. I find I must catch myself by surprise if I am to learn anything surprising.

I believe there is another matter at stake. My self-analysis goes better in a climate I experience as play rather than work. In self-analysis, as in all arts, some practitioners prefer to stress play and to smuggle in the necessities of work; others prefer to stress work and to smuggle in what they regard as play. And, though it seems reasonable to suppose that there must always be a mix of play and work or the end is not art but license on the one hand or drudgery on the other, few practitioners seem to create the same mix or to go about their mixing the same way.

3) Beyond wool-gathering and journal-keeping, my third common source of material for self-analysis—I believe it's the most consistently fruitful—is what I experience in the psychoanalytical situation. I seem to learn most about myself when I try to learn something about someone else. Having described those events elsewhere, especially the visual images I see in those circumstances, I shall not dwell further on them here (Gardner, 1983). I want only to say that in the psychoanalytical situation, as elsewhere, I've found that direct introspection is not my best route to new findings. I need to look outward in order to look inward; I need, that is, to look outward to find ways in which looking outward is looking inward, and looking inward, outward.

Whether my self-analytical efforts begin from one source or the other, I find they generally move along this way:

First, having been caught up in the subject at hand, I seem to spin off in unspoken drifts that, in contrast to spoken associations, trip along more erratically. They show, in particular, richer mixes of visual images and metaphors and quicker shifts back and forth from the one to the other and from these to other ways of picturing.

Second, ideas emerge in what I experience as a counterpoint to the first: once again with a mix of words and images but this time with a shift toward more words and fewer images.

Third, I find myself trying to make sense of some piece or of the whole (which is to say, what I experience as making sense). This phase is much wordier but not always exclusively wordy.

Sometimes, the boundaries between the one phase and the other are clear, sometimes not. Sometimes the substance of the third—the sense-making—seems suddenly no longer a logical conclusion but simply a fresh association that triggers the whole sequence again. In one mood, that is, I feel inclined to regard my interpretations as interpretations, and in another, as associations. In the latter circumstances, I find my interpretations more revealing of the interpreter than the interpreted.

I think it's correct, if odd, to say that often I have the sense that I'm first someone free associating, then someone associating to the associating person's associations, and then the same second someone, in a different and more deliberate mood, considering his (or the other's) associations and the play of the one with the other. There seem to be two someones present and one someone is first in one state and then another. If you suppose this imagined dialogue might in some ways repeat the arrangements of the psychoanalytical situation— both those in which I've been the analysand and those in which I've been the analyst—I suppose you're right, but the conversations I've been able to hear usually involve a larger cast of characters. I can't escape the impression that in self-analysis, as in other moments of talking to ourselves, we're rarely if ever alone. Of talkers and listeners there are many.

Hearing many voices over many years—many voices of the observed and observer—hearing *who* is talking to *whom* about *what* and *how* (i.e., in which style, idiom, grammar, accent, tone, and rhythm) has led me to the view that each of these matters is worth fuller study. I've found it fruitful in self-analysis and in the analysis of others to watch for moments of an abrupt *change of voice*, that is, changes in who is talking, changes in ways of talking, changes in what is being talked about, and changes in the imagined nature of the person talked to. I've come to watch especially for those moments when all or many of these changes take place at once. For solo self-analysis and for assisting the self-analysis of others (I call the latter psychoanalysis), I find these moments of multiple change to be moments of the fullest opportunity. (You may recall that the word opportunity is derived from a Latin word designating the moments when the wind is blowing toward port.)

Over and over, liberating ideas, perhaps especially the most liberating ideas, become enslaving. We see it in art. We see it in music. We see it in literature. We see it in politics. We see it in the hard sciences. We see it in psychology.

Exploring the incidents of the weather "trying to clear," I was struck repeatedly by the strength of my urges to drag in once-fresh but now stale insights from my earlier self-analysis and still earlier psychoanalysis. How ironic that we struggle so hard to learn what needs learning and then in the practice of our art must find *a way to "forget"* what we've learned. To find today's truth, we most forget yesterday's. There is no great harm, and even some value, in learning that the foliage of trees is green. But if we want to paint a picture of a tree today, if we want to catch it as it is in today's light, we must forget that trees are green. If we can manage that feat, we shall find that no tree is entirely green, no tree always green, and some trees are never green. The beginning of the art lies in the difficult task of forgetting how things looked in yesterday's light. Evenly hovering attention, the toleration of uncertainty, the tempering of what Keats called "irritable reaching for fact and reason," all ask a finely tuned capacity to forget.

Having for some time found myself going on in these and other ways in loose if heavy dissertation about the importance of forgetting, I wondered at last if I might unconsciously be claiming that, by performing such sleight of mind, I could avoid the effects of prior experiences, beliefs, biases, frames of reference, and other letters of my alphabet. Indeed, if such clearing of the psychic slate were possible, what would it profit me if, in losing my biases, I lost my bearings?

Surely by "forget" I could not mean forget. What I must mean, I told myself, is that we must learn somehow to act *as if* we've forgotten. Otherwise, we come upon only what we expected to come upon. What I must mean is that when, in the act of seeing, we make our prior knowledge less directly available—when we somehow move it from center-of-awareness to edge—we prepare ourselves, when we can, to come upon fresh examples of what our knowledge had prepared us to find and, even on some occasions, somehow to transcend, in some regard, the limits of that knowledge. Old knowledge, though the friend of the new, is at best an ambivalent friend; and sometimes, having such a friend—to paraphrase the old saying—new knowledge doesn't need an enemy.

Having at last noted that in this monologue I'd changed my way of talking, and having noted in particular that I'd swapped "forget" for "redistribute," I wondered at last why I'd jumped from the clearly paradoxical to the opaquely precise? Did I fancy myself on firmer ground by speaking a geographical lingo? And if by my shift I meant to do something more than comfort myself, did I mean "redistribution of knowledge" as analogy or more? You may recall that when Isakower was asked if he meant "analyzing instrument" as analogy or more, he replied: "Somewhere between the one and the other."

I don't know if what I shall now report will strike you as revealing more the advantages or the disadvantages of the chasing of analogy. But I ask you to go with me through a concatenation of thoughts that, though I know it confounds the abstract with the concrete and otherwise violates several canons both of science and ordinary logic, is nevertheless the route upon which my associations insisted.

Faced repeatedly with the question, "Where does knowledge go when you redistribute it?" I found myself of the repeated and decided conviction that it goes *to the back of my head*. Taking this location as seriously as I could, I observed that it pertained to a very different "edge-of-awareness" from the one I'd long been accustomed to imagine. The customary one was an image of something off to the side, a peripheral vision as it were. Yet, clearly, in my present vision of putting knowledge aside I was experiencing that aside as not to the side but to the back.

Having thus settled the matter of location, I asked myself, on another day, "What is this idea of putting knowledge to the back of your head? Just how do you do that?" The tone of these questions reflected another of those changes of voice I mentioned before. This was no longer a proper self-analytical tone. It was cynical. And in that tone—I know several persons I've come to regard as its prototypical bearers—my questions were meant not as the questions they purported to be but as question-stoppers. On the occasion in question, these pseudo-questions loudly proclaimed by their tone: "Stop it! You're going off the deep end with this reifying of spatial analogies."

To my regret, I talk to myself that way sometimes although I know that nothing kills my self-analysis quicker—and means to, I gather—than this mix of oppressive cynicism and reason. That knowledge notwithstanding, being sorely afflicted at the moment by an uncontrollable fit of rigor, I was happy to drop precipitously my uneasy elaborations of topography. With not even a parenthetical wondering about yet another change of voice, I simply translated my thoughts into other abstractions ("attention cathexes" and the like), and let it go at that.

I was startled therefore when, on still another occasion, the dismissed question gently, though firmly, returned: "How *do* you put knowledge in the back of your head?"

Soon after, as if in answer to this question, I observed myself (and have observed myself since) in the visual midst of a curious fantasy: curious in form and having as its subject, I take it, the exercise of curiosity.

In one of those edge-of awareness images that come and go in a flash, I saw myself as a wide-eyed child, running happily ahead, followed by my parents, sometimes father, sometimes mother. (I've not been able to tell when the one or the other though I imagine it depends on the subject of my inquiry.)

It struck me then that here was how I "redistributed knowledge to the back of my head." I imagined that knowledge no longer my own but the knowledge of my parents behind. In back of my head, so to speak. And by virtue of that imagined division of knowledge, and head, I felt myself freer to run about and to look with fresh eye.

My associations to this transformation into child peripatetic observer—walker or runner and seer—have led me back on one occasion and another to joyful moments of childhood in which I rushed ahead to find things and then back to my parents to report my findings and to benefit from their enthusiasm and knowledgeable commentary. (I persist in the belief that, in the main, my parents entered into those exploratory exchanges with as much excitement as I.)

Probably you've noticed that in the overall sweep of my remarks, my images have gone from recent sky-searchings for lights in the dark, to a solitary child seeking similar lights in the dark, to adult self-analytical searchings for light in the inner dark (moments of opportunity), to imagined redistribution of knowledge, to the child-of-separation seeking other enlightenment with benefit of parent in back, and so on and on in full spirals of distressing darks and pleasing lights.

I did not, of course, consciously plan these details of my itinerary. Rather, they reflect, I think, the strength of the regressive and progressive forces that shape and reshape not only our associative drifts but all our perception, cognition, and action. And they reflect, I think, the evocative and organizing effects of the special configurations one recovers, wants to recover, and can't help but recover in particular states of self-analysis: configurations formed and reformed in dreamlike states, recalled or otherwise reexperienced in dreamlike states, and in the recall, or reexperiencing, evocative of fresh dreamlike states. I mean, of course, slightly dreamlike states.

If I've created the impression that I've found my self-analytical efforts always, or even usually, fruitful, I want now to correct that miscreation. I find self-analysis a most uneven procedure. Often my thoughts seem to lumber along and go nowhere in particular, at least, nowhere in particular I can recognize. "Nowhere in particular" and "no feelings in particular" are among the most familiar landmarks.

Even when self-analytical efforts seem to go without hitch, a second glance reveals many. When I look back at my search of my images of the weather trying to clear and at my afterimages, though I recall that I regarded these efforts, when they took place, as relatively moving bits of self-analysis—moving me and moving rapidly—what impresses me is how slowly each step advanced and, once taken, how quickly and often these steps were reversed. I'm impressed by the scope of what I missed and by the narrowness of my associations and interpretations. This sense in the thick of things of proceeding rapidly and this retrospective sense of slowness and incompleteness seem ubiquitous features. Moreover, anyone else's report of self-analysis often strikes me as much ado about nothing, or, to put it more cautiously, usually leaves me with a similar impression that self-analysis progresses exceedingly slowly and small piece by small piece, *if* it progresses at all.

What seems surprising is not that self-analysis progresses slowly but that self-analysis progresses. Two aspects of our natures seem to favor this occasional, though limited, progress.

First is the fortunate circumstance that defenses and other resistances are neither so consistent nor so solid as we sometimes imagine. In the abstract, we may conceive of structures as *relatively* abiding configurations, but in practice it's all too easy to forget the "relatively." A self-analyzer finds and needs often to refind that defenses and other resistances—like all structures, psychological and physical—have their hidden fluidities. We find and need to refind what we thought we knew: *Nothing in nature is static.*

If sufficiently patient and persistent, we find that we can *sometimes* catch our resistances, especially our defenses, at ebb tide rather than flood. Self-analysis blocked at one hour often moves a bit at another. A defense—or its derivative—completely obstructive at one point, becomes bypassable at another; a defense, invisible at one point, becomes visible at another, visible and even, occasionally, self-analyzable. Self-analysis, I believe, has helped me often to rediscover and explore the defenses I'd earlier discovered in my psychoanalysis, sometimes helped me to discover and explore defenses I'd not earlier discovered, occasionally helped me to discover defenses I'd not discovered before in myself or in others, and, on rare occasions, helped me to discover defenses I'd neither heard of nor thought of before.

Along with the fluidities of our defenses and of other resistances and the resulting chances of observing their workings, there comes to our aid in self-analysis—however quietly—

that obscure phenomenon we call *the thrust toward development*. In assisting my own self-analytical efforts and in assisting the self-analytical efforts of others – that is, as analyst to myself and to others – and in examining other spoken and unspoken flights of imagination, I've been struck by how elaborately and persistently the thrust toward development expresses itself in edge-of-awareness self-analytical efforts, or what I prefer to call edge-of-awareness inquiries. I have the impression that conscious self-analysis, when most effective, joins forces with those ongoing, leading-edge, half-hidden, or latent inquiries essential to our development. Those edge-of-awareness inquiries, those questions both universal and particular, are always expressed and disguised in our *highly individual codes;* and those questions and those codes always shape and are shaped by both reactionary and progressive intentions.

A ssuming it in some respects possible, of what value is self-conscious pursuit of self-analysis?
    Even a cursory review of the literature reveals the expectable divergence of views. Self-analysis is lauded as promising the most remarkable possibilities and scorned as, by definition, impossible. Arguments are particularly sharp over the therapeutic possibilities of self-analysis. You know these extremes; I'll not discuss them now. But I do want to say of our expectations that there seems a ditch on both sides of the road: expecting too much and expecting too little.

Most psychoanalysts would agree that the line is thin between self-analysis and self-deception. I know some who maintain that there is no line. To those who say self-analysis is impossible I can only reply that, if we gave up all activities we know to be impossible, life would be impossibly impoverished.

I suppose we might learn more about the therapeutic value of self-analysis when and if we have the benefit of many samples of the efforts of many persons over short runs and long, and when and if we have a satisfactory way to explore how these persons have or have not changed. We shall then face the knotty problem of assessing how our method of assessing has or has not changed what we're assessing.

You'll correctly suspect from what I've said and how I've said it that I imagine we'll sooner come to the view that in matters of such complexity, it's highly unlikely there are simple sequences deserving consideration as cause and effect. We are, after all, almost in the 21st century.

In my own case, I believe that the long and fanatical pursuit of self-analysis has brought about no discernable improvements in my character, and no more than occasional small gains in tension management, in self–object differentiation, in solidifying self-esteem, in resolution of intra-psychic conflicts, and in advancing homespun creative capabilities.

Even if therapeutic gains were considerably greater, I see no reason to confine self-analytical endeavors to the therapeutic, nor to confine them to the alchemic conversion of countertransference burdens into useful insights, nor even to the maintaining and advancing of evenly hovering attention, all of which might reasonably be touted by and for those analysts of a utilitarian turn of mind. In my view, for involvement in so conspicuously inefficient and demanding a procedure as self-analysis, the best justification is that it's *fun*. To paraphrase George Bernard Shaw's review of a play, this is an activity that will be liked by those who like this sort of activity.

Yet I want now to depart sufficiently from this hedonistic position to say something more about the potential self-analytical advantages to which I alluded earlier.

If we follow my weather images and my fantasies of redistribution of knowledge one way, they reflect, in both content and form, specific old and ongoing disturbances of my nature. But followed another way, it seems to me, they reflect efforts each of us makes, in ways specific to each, to recreate conditions, real and imagined, each finds salutory for many ends.

My "redistribution of knowledge" seems both a way to "forget" and a way not to "forget," a way to let go and a way not to let go. Of course. Freud said it all along. We never really let go. We only find, when we can, new forms for the old. Others have said the same. Everything changes, but all remains the same. Nothing changes, but all is different.

My fantasy of redistribution of knowledge seems one of those never-ending efforts to have things both ways, to throw out neither the baby nor the bath water, neither, that is, the baby nor its supportive surround. My imagined division of cognition between self and parents creates in my mind *a mind-clearing illusion of "forgetting,"* an illusion that assures me, all in the same moment, that the knowledge still guides me — won't let me get lost — and if and when needed will be available on request. (Request, in this dialect, is surely a euphemism for demand.)

I find, over and over, that my visions of pleasurable childhood comings and goings, separations and returns (and other pleasurable findings of light in the dark) seem to soothe the pains of separation from familiar knowledge, especially *personified knowledge* to which I'd previously clung. I find, over and over, that they soothe the pains of *other separations and other changes of orientation*, present and past, inner and outer, shallow and deep. I find, over and over, visions of *painful* partings from persons, places, and things delicately balanced by visions of *pleasing* partings. And I find, over and over, that my ways of letting go are my ways of holding on. Each object, each function I glimpse, proves a bridge from there to here, from past to present, from inner to outer.

I find, over and over, both comfort and challenge in seeing in my head or seeing in my surround, today's lights in the dark; I find comfort and challenge in my particular ways of imagining and seeing (favorite colors, shapes, tonal juxtapositions, etc.). In visual play in general, and with lights and darks in particular, I find my mind most frisky and most exploratory. I find that in the look of a ray of sunlight on an old stone wall, in the twinkle of colors in the shadow of a dune, in the tension between a gleam in the eye and a dark scowl, my mind leaps about (when I can follow the leaps) and seems to have no trouble finding apparent connections between this seemingly limited microcosm of current visual impression and the seemingly endless preoccupations—conflicts, interests, and other occupants of my mind—that press for expression.

Proceeding from the assumption that what I've observed of myself is not entirely idiosyncratic, let me try now to frame some generalizations. I shall put them as statements, but I mean them as questions:

As we go back and forth in time and space, each has preferred ways of *touching home base*. When in slightly dreamlike states, we suspend some functions and sharpen others; when we turn our worlds upside down and, in the turning, enlighten and frighten ourselves, each has his or her own ways of making the unfamiliar familiar.

In these epiphanies—Wordsworth called them "spots of time"—we go home again both by what we conjure and by our very ways of conjuring.

Having organized our first self–other worlds in our own idiosyncratic ways of seeing, hearing, thinking, and other ways of figuring, we expand those worlds from the most familiar to other and larger worlds—from mother, for example, to Mother Nature—our exercise of these familiar functions helps each of us to find, that is, to construct, in the face of extraordinary change, an extraordinary array of constancies and continuities. In this sense, we can, and always do, go home again. *We cannot go forward without going back.* We go home not simply through what we perceive in the world away from home but in the very act of elaborating the ways of perceiving we once exercised solely at home, and, in particular, in elaborating our familiar and highly individual ways of perceiving. All this, I imagine, forever creates new versions of child immigrant to new worlds.

We find the worlds we seek, and we find them in the particular ways we seek to find them. As John Berger (1980) once put it, "The field that you are standing before appears to have the same proportions as your own life" (p. 198).

I take it that all our seekings and searchings are reflected in our seemingly simplest perceptions; if we could and would associate freely to our everyday perceptions, we could and would find that in many regards those perceptions are as much a dream as those dreams we dream asleep. If every dream is full of day residues, every perception is full of dream residues.

I take it that this ordinary interdigitation—this interpenetration, this endless conversion of inner to outer to inner to outer—is even more complex in those special worlds of perception in which each of us most fully chooses, and cannot help choosing, to live. To those who make their worlds most rich by what they touch and by what touches them, one such perception, memory, metaphor, or other image of touching is more touching than a thousand perceptions, memories, metaphors, or other images otherwise figured. Let Proust have the smell of his madeleines; they will have the touch.

When once we know these favorite experiential codes of ourselves or another, we know where in our self analyses or in our analyses of others to attend most carefully to grasp what most moves us or the other. We know, too, the tongue in which we must talk to talk most movingly to ourselves or another.

Some persons have confided in me that in their reveries, and other progressive-regressions (for example, in states of evenly hovering attention), they routinely see things; others that they hear things; others that they feel things. Only one person has spoken of smelling things. No one has yet told me of tasting things. Most of us use many ways but subspecialize in some in particular.

One woman revealed not only that she customarily feels things but that she feels them in what she takes to be a particular part of her gut. Thus, when she has a "gut feeling" about something, it's really a gut feeling. I know a man who feels things mainly in his large muscles. I know another who gets his messages most richly in proprioceptive sensations.

One man revealed a consistent series of visual images in which I was able to discern a special sensitivity to an extraordinary range of details of perspective and of the complex relations of near objects to far. Another heard things in ways that put special stress—described though unrecognized—on nuances of volume and pitch, especially on subtle contrasts of volume and pitch, quick and slight juxtapositions of louds and softs, highs and lows. He fathomed what people meant as much or more from these musical particulars as from the content of their words.

I've been struck by how often the preference for a particular perceptual system is matched by a preference for metaphors constructed of the materials of that system and, within it, of preferred subsystems. And I've been struck by how often the boundaries between the preferred perception and the preferred metaphor are unclear. When some persons say, "I see what you mean," they mean what they say. They are not talking metaphor; they are talking actuality.

We know of this phenomenon in psychotics and even in those we say have a vivid imagination, are visual thinkers, use eidetic imagery, and the like. But I suspect that these experiences are more common to the rest of us than we know. And I wonder what kinds of confusion result when the person who hears things and the one who feels things talk to each other and each thinks the other is talking metaphor when the other is not.

I believe—which means I have a hunch—that in self-analysis, as in other arts, when we descend into those states in which our preferred metaphors, images, and perceptions shift most fluidly from the one to the other, we are most where for us "the action is." Which is also to say I suspect that, for most of us, creativity is liveliest where the boundary narrows most between creativity and confusion. We cannot choose the terms of our creativity. It is necessary, as the old Texas saying tells us, to "dance with them that brung ya."

Though I agree with those analysts who've said that our most adaptive functions tend to be most silent and therefore most difficult to observe, I wonder if those functions would seem quite so silent if in listening to ourselves, and to others, we were tuned less selectively to the sounds of malady. And, if in our states of what we hope to be *progressive regression,* we were to observe more carefully the contents of our preferred means and conditions of perception and representation, if we were to pursue those observations more vigorously, take them more seriously, and share them more candidly, I wonder if self-analysis might make a more consistent, recognizable, and valuable contribution to the variegated fields of adult observation. I wonder, especially, if a fuller sharing of our observations of our preferences of perception and of representation, and of our accompanying fantasies, might tell us more about those functions, about the intricacies of separation and restitution, and about the elusive workings of the creativity of everyday life. I refer to the earliest creativities of our childhood and to those later creativities that repeat, elaborate, and transcend the earlier.

In self-analysis, I believe, some aspects of our common functioning, that is, of our functioning in common, become, through different quirks of our natures, more visible to some of us and other aspects to others. *We have, one might say, different holes in our heads;* and these permit different looks inward at what, in one form or another, may pertain to us all. If we could bear telling more and hearing more, it seems plausible to expect an advance in our common knowledge.

Even if I'm mistaken in these expectations of general advance, I believe such pursuits of self-inquiry might have the individual benefit of sharpening our sensitivities to the endless subjectivities in what we ordinarily regard objectivities. If nothing else, the expanded search of the relation between the observer and the observed—for example, between ourselves and what *we* observe—might help us to achieve a laudable, if limited, increase of humility. In this regard, however, we are forewarned by Benjamin Franklin, who, in the conclusion to his *Autobiography* says that the reader can now see what a struggle he, Mr. Franklin, has waged to achieve a proper humility. But the trouble, he adds, is that it's so easy to become inordinately proud of one's humility.

AFTERTHOUGHTS

This paper was written in 1986 and was presented in slightly varying forms at meetings of the Philadelphia, Cleveland, and

Western New England Psychoanalytic Societies. It was later published in its present form in a collection called *Self Analysis: Critical Inquiries, Personal Visions* (Barron, 1993).

By this time, I had made it a practice to take periodic soundings of my reactions outside the analytic situation, soundings similar to those I had been taking inside. (See the extraanalytic instance at the outset of this paper.) Whatever the gain of the one sounding or the other—sometimes larger, sometimes lesser—I had found over time that the extraanalytic soundings aided the intraanalytic and vice versa. I had also found that my most fruitful inquiries in each situation began frequently, perhaps usually, with a visual experience. That renewed awareness of my visual proclivities had led me increasingly to try to identify the favorite perceptual modes that provide other persons—patients and analysts in particular—the most promising points of departure for their self-inquiries.

I had come to accept as a given the ubiquity and strength of the human inclination toward self-inquiry and the importance of that inclination as a potential vehicle of the thrust toward development. This paper reflected ongoing efforts to identify not only the starting points but the ensuing content and form—genres of inquiry—employed characteristically, if largely unknowingly, by one person and another in pursuit of their hidden questions. These efforts to identify preferred genres of inquiry were, at the time, fast becoming key elements in my approach both to analyzing and to teaching, that is, in my efforts to assist the self-inquiries of patients and students, however different that assistance might necessarily be, given the different aims of analytic and nonanalytic education. In turn, I found myself trying increasingly to observe ways in which the hidden questions of analysts and patients, of teachers and students, and of other participants in other pairings shape the exchanges between them and serve both to advance and to obstruct the hidden questions of each.

As a consequence of these and other studies, I found myself of the view that analyzing and teaching, whatever else they might be, could usefully be regarded as efforts to assist in the advance of hidden questions, hidden questions of the analyst and the patient and the teacher and the student. I found myself, that is, of the view that although analyzing and teaching may do more, they do well when they do no less than assist in the advance of the hidden questions of the participants. And, as I look back, it seems clearer than it did at the time that I was trying more and more to find ways in which the advance of my patients', my students', and my own hidden questions might be assisted, or at least, if possible, not obstructed.

Chapter Seven

===================

RECOLLECTIONS
Sexuality, Neurosis, and Analysis

L ast summer in Paris, I suddenly spoke French. I spoke, that is, a different French.

Earlier in the summer and in earlier summers, I'd spoken the memorized words, phrases, and sentences I customarily trot out in the average predictable circumstances for which they'd laboriously been learned. Such French isn't all bad. For securing food, lodging, transportation, and other tourist necessities and comforts, it's sometimes better than no French at all.

But one day last summer I threw caution to the winds, departed from my habitual routines, and came up with a few winged sentences I'd never used or heard before. In some way—the precise workings of which I was, and am still, unaware—I used words that, till I used them, I didn't know I knew and combined words as I'd never combined words before. I found myself concocting, however timidly and briefly, a few of those mixes of the expected and unexpected that come, if they come, only after we've carefully learned, carefully forgot, part recovered, and part transcended, the elementary schemes with which we began. Voila! I'd made the mysterious leap from thinking and speaking Applied French to thinking and speaking French.

When I reflect on the changes in my theories of disorder and my ways of analyzing, the changes that come first to mind—I suspect they belong first—seem similar. When I was a beginner, I spoke mainly Applied Analysis. Somewhere along the way, I think I began to speak more of that peculiar and less clearly definable mix I now regard as analysis.

It's hard to be sure about such extravagant claims, the urge being strong to rewrite history and near irresistible to show that yesterday's errors, recognized and corrected, have led to today's wisdoms. I'll try to resist.

We on the panel have been invited to tell our views of the role of sexuality in neurosogenesis, how over the years these views have changed, and how such changes of view have changed how we practice.

We've been invited to illustrate these changes by telling of an analysis past and how we'd proceed if it were an analysis present.

I want to say right off that I don't think my changes can be said to be changes of theory leading to changes of method. I think one change lies in there being fewer linear connections between my theories and methods, in one direction or the other. And if linear may be somewhat at stake, the direction, I think, has been not so much from change of theory to change of practice but more the other way round: from change of practice to change of theory. (I'm speaking, of course, of subjective reality—that is, of how I've experienced the changes.)

Besides, I can't say, except in broad outline, that yesterday I analyzed one way and today I'd do it another. That inability, I believe, is another piece of the change. Yesterday, I think I might have predicted how I'd proceed in one situation or another and how, given the chance, I'd redo something already done. Today, what seems predictable is that I'm less predictable. Or I hope to be. Today, I consider suspect many kinds of predictability that yesterday I did not. Today, stance seems properly more predictable, particulars less. (I want to mention the matter of stance now and come back to it later.)

The difference between a direct, largely conscious translation of what experience and theory tell us and an indirect, largely preconscious, freshly evolving expression—a disciplined unpredictability—is hard to observe and harder to describe. But that difference seems to me key to the best constancies and the best changes in our method. The difference between stale application and lively recreation, (or new creation), may be what Mark Twain had in mind when, in his pithy if chauvinistic way, he said of his wife's profanity, "Right words; wrong tune."

I imagine we'd agree that, in telling of what we do, we confound both by excess ambiguity and by imprecise precision. I don't want to suggest more unpredictability and indirection in our method than is the case, but neither do I want to obscure the friskiness of play among theory, knowledge, understanding, and practice, nor the delicate and desirable tortuosity of line between what we did yesterday and what we do today.

Technique that does not, in its particulars, take the technician by surprise is surprisingly poor technique; our classical method relies heavily on jazz. But it's precisely the difficulty of translating that music into words that makes telling what we do—especially how we put belief into action—so often seem, at best, desiccated, at worst, deceptive.

Nevertheless, I'll try to tell a) some ways I practice, or at least look at things today, b) some ways these ways seem different from yesterday's, and c) some ways my notions of neurosogenesis, of analytical aims, and of analytical means seem to have changed ensemble.

I'll talk mainly of practices first and theories later, and of changes in the former leading to changes in the latter; but I assume we agree that changes in the one spur, and are spurred, by changes in the other and that talk of one thing leading directly to another is at best a useful fiction, a fiction that ceases to be useful if, in actual practice, it becomes fact. (I assume we also agree that, although, as in any discipline, some aspects of practice lag behind theory and some aspects of theory lag behind practice, art, in the main, goes far ahead of theory and it's theory's job to try persistently to close the gap.)

Nearly 40 years ago, while a resident at the New York Psychiatric Institute, I was seated one day behind a patient who was seated by a window looking out on Riverside Drive. I'd contrived this strange arrangement to aid and abet what I understood to be free association, and to do so without the use of a couch, which it seemed not cricket to use since I was not at that time an analyst.

After a while I was struck and remarked to my patient that her thoughts turned repeatedly round the possibility of an auto accident. She seemed startled by this observation. She began to tell of other dangers, current and past, at home and abroad. Returning, however, to what I took to be her most lively fear of the moment, I asked whether she had any idea what might be making her especially worried about auto accidents. Learning that she did not, I offered the opinion that there might have been such an accident in her past.

I'd read Breuer and Freud's (1895) *Studies on Hysteria*, you see, and I was prepared to find that the repression of a memory of a traumatic event, and a consequent blockage of feelings, was the source of my patient's neurosis. In those days of that residency, we received none of the currently popular supervision. Rather, we proceeded in psychotherapy—if we proceeded—whichever way we were inclined. I considered myself a Freudian.

To my disappointment, my patient replied that she'd *never* been involved in an auto accident. Having learned, however, that there were no negatives in the unconscious, I asked her to consider the possibility that she was mistaken. She assured me her experiences in cars were uniformly pleasing and safe. Then, having documented her assertion by telling of long and delightful rides in the country with her father—a driver of unquestionable excellence in whose company she always felt comfortable and safe—she suddenly recalled with surprise and pain that she had, indeed, been in an auto accident long forgot.

She said between sobs that years earlier she'd been engaged in intercourse with her boy friend on the back seat of his car and his condom had broken; moreover, as a consequence, she said, she'd rushed into her present miserable marriage. After several weeks of daily sessions of what I regarded laudable abreaction of pent-up emotions, she pronounced herself free of the claustro- and agoraphobias for which she'd been admitted to the hospital. And after careful deliberation by the appropriate authorities, she was soon discharged as cured.

I was amazed by this "proof" of the validity of Freud's theories of neurosogenesis and by the remarkably curative effects of his free association method. Though this was the late 1940s, I was familiar only, and not very clearly, with his 1895 trauma theory of neurosogenesis, his abreaction theory of therapeutic aims, and his catharsis theory of cure. I didn't know that he'd since changed his theories and methods. In treating this patient, and others, I found the early Freud—that is, my Freud—an extraordinarily helpful supervisor.

It's all very well to be amused by the antics of beginners. But it seems to me a virtue of beginners that they show crudely and transparently the problems with which the rest of us struggle, though perhaps more subtly, forever. With my accident patient I was, of course, not simply attentive to, but *driving*, her associative drift (if we can call it an associative drift). And I was doing so with the help of a theory of neurosogenesis, and of analytic aims and means, whose limitations were compounded by my too literal translation of theory—ill digested theory—into practice.

Yet, in this happening, I seem to have applied some smattering of the free association method and of the evenly hovering attention it asks; which seems to have helped me to apprehend her concern and to remark on it at a moment of opportunity; which seems to have invited, or supported, her rediscovering and reliving of an auto accident, even if not quite the accident I had in mind.

It is now clear, of course, though it was not then, that my

approximate attunement and debatable insistence had a fair chance of striking a responsive note, given the nature of her character, of our relationship, of the metaphor-making capacities of the human mind, and of the breadth of human experience. (There is no shortage of "accidents" in life, of course, and no shortage of ways to represent them.)

The never-ending discovery of such curious mixes of correctness and error reminds us repeatedly that ours *is* an impossible profession. Yet I imagine we'd agree that to claim ours is more impossible than others would be an unwarranted conceit. Whatever our professions, theories, and methods, surely we're all, at best, somewhat right and somewhat wrong.

Within a year or so, I'd changed my views of what my patient had most likely been experiencing with me, her backseat psychiatrist. And having begun to wonder who was doing what to whom; I soon saw this therapy as a case of substituting new accidents for old.

Moreover, within a year or so, I'd learned something of unconscious sexual and aggressive wishes, the unconscious distresses to which they give rise, and the unconscious means we use to gratify those wishes and avoid those distresses. Delighted with this expansion of theory, and with what promised to be an expansion of know-how, I then proceeded with an "evenly" hovering attention attuned especially to derivatives of those subterranean forces. (I even had the good fortune to see this patient again and to see her in this dawning new light.)

The change proved useful. But if the content of my theory and the focus of my attention had changed—and for the better, I think—it seems to me, as I look back, that the constriction of the free association method, and of evenly hovering attention, largely remained. I was at risk, I think, of trading old Procrustean couches for new.

The line between a useful theory and a monomania is disconcertingly narrow. In principle, we might readily agree that our theories should be taken, as Niebuhr said religious persons should take their myths: "seriously, but not too seriously." Yet such reasonability is a tall order. Problems never cease.

Now, looking back, it seems to me that my early and precipitous shift from one theory and therapeutic method to another, and my early untutored experiments with what I regarded to be the free association method, did at least help to jolt both my interest in the nature of the instrument by which we gather the data that inform and are informed by our theories and my interest in the connections between my nature and the nature of my favored theories and means. And I believe these experiences encouraged some habits of mind that have led over the years to changes in my analytical methods and theories, a few of which I'll try now to sketch.

Of the changes in my work that seem to count most, most arise, I believe, or at least crystalize, from self-analysis, or what, to mark it more sharply from psychoanalysis, I prefer to call self-inquiry.

My involvement in self-inquiry, my fuller involvement, began innocently enough (if anything can be said to begin innocently enough). To explore the uneven workings of my "evenly" hovering attention, I undertook some years ago an inward look at that attention and at the states in which it occurs. I've tried elsewhere (Gardner, 1983) to describe that effort and I'll not repeat the undertaking here. But I do want to say that what began as a sporadic experiment has since become a habit; and that habit has steadily, unexpectedly, and repeatedly changed.

At first I focused on impediments to my evenly hovering attention (especially countertransference and other blind spots). But gradually my attention fanned out to other events: analytical and extra, adaptive and mal. Over and over, by one or another means, I found myself drawn to one or another spot—trouble or not—where the borders between my inner and outer worlds are conspicuously thin: which is also to say, where the borders are thin between psychopathology and richer possibility. Though days at first seemed odd when I was in this way lost and found, days when I'm not now seem even odder.

One thing leads to another and another. Yet if one technical consequence stands out, I'd say it's that I've become more superficial. Or, to put it more charitably, I seem to have become more impressed by the depth of what I once regarded surface. Today, both in my self-inquiries and in my analytical work, I find myself traversing longer and longer and more and more twisted paths before reaching what yesterday I regarded neurosogenenic essence. And now, when I arrive wherever it is I arrive, I'm considerably less sure what is, and what is not, genesis.

Causal chains grow longer. Straight lines become spirals. Epigenesis becomes more epi.

I imagine that this aspect of my ontogeny recapitulates the phylogeny of our field. But, as is the case with any ontogeny, some strands seem a bit idiosyncratic. If, as I suppose, many of us now pay more attention to what yesterday seemed surface, we seem to differ considerably in the areas we prefer as gateway and path to whatever we consider depth.

I, for example, on becoming more involved in the pursuit of my self-inquiries, found myself attending more to my patient's self-inquiries. By self-inquiries I refer not to the limited self-conscious inquiries in which some of us are sometimes involved but to the more elusive, fuller, *almost-but-not-quite-conscious inquiries* in which all of us, I believe, are always involved.

I've come to assume that whatever else we might consciously and unconsciously be doing, we are—in ways of which we're usually but dimly, if at all, aware—always pursuing edge-of-awareness inquiries essential to our growth and development. I mean I've come to assume that we're always trying *both* to advance *and* to retard those unwitting inquiries and the thrusts of development they serve.

I've come to expect that sometimes—sometimes we might call creative—these largely hidden or latent inquiries heighten, broaden, and deepen. I consider the analytical situation among those "sometimes." In my view, we don't inquire because we're in analysis; we're in analysis because we inquire.

Seen so, analysis works by expanding some of those salient covert inquiries in which, in analysis or not, we're all persistently involved. Seen so, analysts, with occasional good-enough empathy, intuition, understanding, timing, and tact and using one means and theory and another—some means and some theories more usefully than others—assist in the advance of those hidden inquiries (our patients' and our own). I think we so assist occasionally; I think things generally go better when we do; I think, all things being equal (of course they rarely are), things go better when we blend the content and the form of our analytical perceptions and interventions with the content and form of both our patient's and our own almost-but-not-quite-recognized inquiries. (When and how we aid the advance, and when and how we obstruct, deserves, I think, more consideration than it can now be given.)

What has all this to do with sexuality and neurosogenesis? It leads there. Slowly.

I find the routes followed by these inquiries good routes—I'm not much a believer in royal routes—to the unconscious workings of the mind; that is, I find them good routes to those unities of inner and outer world by which such inquiries are endlessly shaped and which they endlessly shape. Followed one way, our inquiries reflect those great questions of existence that forever preoccupy philosophers, playwrights, poets, painters, and others of that ilk. Followed another way, they lead to those underworld particulars that most interest us as analysts.

Self-inquiries are often soft spoken. (Or perhaps we listeners are hard of hearing.) Even when audible, self-inquiries often seem unpromising: too narrow or too broad, too philosophical or not philosophical enough, too concrete or too abstract, too charged or not charged enough.

A patient goes on day after day in what seem reality-bound dreams and other associations about household repairs. Nothing seems addressable till it can gradually be grasped that he's passionately involved in an extraordinary range of questions about how to attach one thing to another: whether by adhesive or by nail or screw, whether by joinings that adhere tightly or loosely, whether by dovetailing or simpler abutting, whether temporarily or more permanently, whether by this or that reversible or relatively irreversible means. (It's remarkable how large a world can be joined—joined passionately—to the seemingly small world of joinery.) I imagine you can imagine the range of questions then salient. But you cannot imagine how often and assiduously he pursued these and other inquiries, in metaphor and actuality, using the many dialects of carpentry.

I've promised not to rerun an analysis. And I'll not. I'll not even rerun the piece of preanalytical work about which I earlier reminisced.

But I think I can say that, if I were working today with my accident patient, much would seem different. I'd attend more, I imagine, to the tension between her urges and her fears of "driving" with father, and with other "drivers" (including myself), and to her ways of gratifying those urges and avoiding those fears. And I don't see how I could fail to attend more to the preoedipal prologues and postoedipal epilogues to those "driving" concerns. I'd assume, that is, that my patient's auto eroticism took a long and complicated trip.

But, if it can be said that present theories of neurosogenesis would urge me to attend today to some matters that yesterday I did not, I think it can as well be said I'd attend more to those, and other, matters because I'd be less concerned with neurosogenesis. Or perhaps I should say I'd be less consciously concerned and, consciously or not, less exclusively.

Today, for example, I'm struck—as I was not then—by the strength and the scope of her preoccupations not only with danger but, in the context of danger and beyond, with motion. In fact, today her concern—her fascination—with motion seems to me major, and her preoccupation with danger, a movable piece. That small shift in my attention, I suspect, might not be of small consequence to her and to me.

Observed in review, she now seems to me to have lived life

most abundantly (most joyfully and fearfully) in the actualities and metaphors of walking, skipping, running, dancing, jumping, skiing, riding, and other erotic mobilities. She seems endlessly preoccupied with the soothing, exciting, and frightening aspects of these motions and their threatened cessations. (She was, in fact, a dancer; she was in fancy either about to take off in new mobilities or to bog down precipitously in astasia abasia and other dramatic immobilities.)

Today, I'm struck by the ingenuity with which, in the genre of motion, she both pursued and obstructed her inquiries. She seems to me to have used thoughts of slow motion both to avoid thoughts of rapid motion and to edge toward and accentuate the rapid by reaching it by way of the slow. (Some techniques of both choreography and cinematography come to mind.) She seems to think of "safe" rides with father *both* not to think of "dangerous" rides *and* to pave the way for thoughts of "safes" that turn out to be dangers. Thoughts of movements in "front" seats and "back" seats seem to move away from and toward each other and away from and toward the anatomical parts and inquiries I now imagine they'd have revealed had I understood and helped her to understand her code.

Today, I'm struck that my patient was a cartographer of motion. She seems persistently to have been mapping in her mind places where dangers—especially of accelerated motion in out-of-control vehicles and slowed motion in exitless spaces and crowded places—are most likely and least likely to be found. (Some maps of ancient cartographers come to mind: the ones with the sea serpents, whirlpools, and other terrestrial and aquatic dangers.)

Today, I see her fascination with the moving dangers of her outer world not only as efforts to avoid what she found dangerous in her inner, but as efforts—however preliminary, tentative, and tangential—to inquire at safe distance into the dangers of the inner. Today, I'd regard her preoccupations with movement, danger, and mapping as serving, with much artistry, phobic purposes and larger ends.

Today, I'd regard my patient as one of those persons for whom the most moving matters are *literally* most moving.

Today, therefore, in following her edge-of-awareness inquiries, I imagine I'd be led not only to the pleasures and risks of rocking, reaching out, grabbing hold, letting go, sitting up, sitting down, taking a stand, going forth, going back and forth and up and down (and to the solo, two-party, and more-party activities of which these motions would be found singly and in combinations to be part), but also to her many efforts to apply old solutions and find new solutions to the many dilemmas posed by her antithetical moving inclinations.

A nalyzing patients is easy. Analyzing where it counts is what's hard.

To follow the lead of almost-but-not-quite-recognized inquiries seems to me a good way to work from the surface, to begin at points of manifest conflict, to follow the affect, to analyze where transference and resistance are lively and accessible, and to apply other well-known rules of thumb that help a bit to analyze where it counts. To search for ways in which both free association and evenly hovering attention are organized by an ego both driving and driven, both advancing and retreating, seems part of tried and true notions of compromise formation, overdetermination, and multiple function. To explore persistently—whether or not I think I'm in trouble—the play of a patient's self-inquiries and my own seems one with the analytical habit of looking at things neither alone as interpersonal nor intrapsychic but now as one and now the other and, occasionally, with that double vision that all at once sees them as both. I assume you find this terrain thoroughly familiar even if my particular approach may in some regards be foreign.

We do not acquire our ways and theories by inheritance, but by industry. Within our common framework, each of us builds his or her own theories and methods; and each of those theories and methods is at least as personal as theoretical.

Once, when Helene Deutsch had reached what some call a "certain age," she was asked at a conference on aging to say a few words. "I know what you want to know," she said. "You want to know what it's like to be old. I'll tell you. When you're old, you're the way you were when you were young, only more so."

I suppose so. And I suppose the same is true of our growth as analysts. Yet these "more-so's" may add up at some point—for good, bad, or both—not simply to changes of degree but changes of kind. (I'll not belabor the parallels in the world of physical science.)

A full discussion of the scope, gains, and losses of "more so's" would be unbearable and irrelevant. But I do want to say that I believe that following, or trying to follow, the play of my patients' and my self-inquiries helps me, on the average, to attain an evenly hovering attention somewhat more even. I therefore regard my present approach as the one in which I presently prefer to make and search for my mistakes.

When I follow the lead of my patients' and my almost-but-not-quite-recognized inquiries, I find my attention drawn to dilemmas and challenges of tension management, self-object differentiation, self-esteem regulation, the establishment of basic trust, autonomy, initiative and other ego virtues, the advance of capacities for symbolic and abstract thinking, the taming of affect storms to signals, the transition from dyadic to triadic relationships, the resolution of intrapsychic conflicts, and many etceteras. One problem lies in the number and complexity of etceteras, and another in how to regard their relationship to each other and to our analytical purposes.

In analysis, as elsewhere, it's hard to gauge whether the exploration of new complexities is essential, or even useful, to the tasks at hand or whether such expansions of attention trade economy of means for a shallow eclecticism. It's hard to tell what's evenly hovering and what's scattered attention, and, if scattered, whether defensively or for other purposes or causes.

Which brings me at long last to the explicit question of how I view today the role of sexuality in neurosogenesis. I hope you will judge that up to this point I've at least been dealing with the question implicitly.

Whenever and wherever I follow the lead of my patients' and

my self-inquiries, I find I'm led over and over from covert to overt tensions of sexuality. Perhaps that's what I find because that's what I'm looking for. But so be it. That's what I find. And I find that when I help my patients and me to explore such tensions, they and I usually find it beneficial.

I prefer a theory, therefore, that asserts the ubiquity and the importance of sexuality. Some analytical theories of neurosogenesis seem too narrow, some too broad, none just right. Given that choice, I opt for a theory that's a bit too broad. By theories of neurosogenesis, I'm referring to our clinical theories, that is, interlocking theories of disorder, of analytical aims, and of analytical means. (In contrast, general theories of neurosogenesis are at liberty to be as broad as they like and to go back at least as far as Adam and Eve.)

I prefer a theory that asserts the ubiquity and importance of tensions of sexuality but does not deal exclusively with sexuality: a theory, that is, that does deal exclusively with sexuality but does so both narrowly and broadly. I prefer a theory that treats tension management, self–object differentiation, self-esteem regulation and the other etceteras I mentioned (and the many I did not) as essential to the development of sexuality and that treats sexuality as essential to those and other seemingly separate lines of development. I prefer a theory, for example, that portrays in one panorama the play between unfolding capacities for tension management and the unfolding press of salient sexual drives rather than a theory that sketches one set of developments here and the other there, where rarely, if ever, the twain shall meet.

That theory—that preferred theory—would treat relatively autonomous developments as more "relatively" than autonomous and treat relatively separate lines of development as more inseparable than separate. That theory, while ego-ish, would be more id-ish than ego-ish and would locate sexuality in hyphenated unity of sexuality-aggression and would highlight that unity and its many combinations and permutations in its subtheory of genesis and epigenesis of neurosis and of all other accomplishments of the mind.

I prefer a theory that stresses unconscious compromises:

stresses both the compromises born of intrapsychic conflict and the compromises born of other antithetical inclinations, stresses the perpetual play of one with the other, and stresses consistently the play of earlier and later contributing developments. (It's one thing to espouse in principle a concept of epigenesis, another to take the espousal seriously. We may accept in theory the notion of epigenesis, but the seductive appeal of homunculus theories always abides.)

I prefer a theory that does not assert or imply that if we analyze the earlier developments the later will take care of themselves, or if we analyze the later the earlier will take care of themselves. I prefer a theory that posits that we cannot effectively analyze one without analyzing the other. I prefer a theory that doesn't divide us into persons stuck in, or advanced to, one era or another but, rather, while specifying individual variations and preponderances, portrays all of us struggling in common, each in his or her own particular way, in that broad range from our finest hours to our relatively rare, or relatively frequent, psychoses of everyday life.

I prefer a theory that guides my attention, but does so gently. I prefer a theory that's simple enough to remember and complex enough to "forget." (I mean, of course, a theory simple and complex enough to learn, forget, rediscover, and transcend.)

Do we now have such a theory? I think so. That is, I think we almost but not quite have such a theory.

Analysts may begin by discussing the price of peanut brittle in British Columbia, but they soon will be discussing the Oedipus Complex. Let's hope so. The question is, how shall we discuss it?

One of my teachers, Ives Hendrick, used to say, "Don't tell me the patient has an Oedipus Complex; tell me which kind." Of course.

It seems to me that telling "which kind" would today include telling more fully of the re-creations within the Oedipus complex—repetitive and transcendental, regressive and progressive—of the tensions and configurations of earlier eras. The more things change, the more they remain the same; nothing changes, but all things are different.

I've found no reason to foresake the view that, for most patients we call neurotic and most we call by less flattering names, oedipal developments comprise nodal reorganizations. I've found no reason to foresake the view that re-creations of oedipal events hold for most patients unique analytical possibilities. I suppose, therefore, I could be called an analytical oedipalist.

But, of course, much depends on what we regard as "oedipal." Today, more than yesterday, I take the view that preoedipal developments that unfold in the analytical situation— regressions, fixations, arrests, and the like—are not regrettable obstacles to, but essential elements of, the oedipal. Today, it seems to me, I'm not faced, as I once thought, with the job of analyzing either the oedipal or the preoedipal, nor the one first and the other later, but, in the main, of analyzing the earlier within and becoming the later. (That's another piece of what I mean by analyzing where it counts.)

Today I find that following my patients' and my edge-of-awareness inquiries, and the transferences and resistances by which they're shaped and shape, repeatedly points up the surprisingly fluid nature of our natures. What clearly seems castration anxiety at one point reveals a fear of loss of body boundaries at another and a fear of flooding by ill-defined tensions at still another, and more often than not characteristic mixes and sequences of the one and the other. What appears as a clear oedipal passion at one point reveals at another that, as the old saying has it, we don't know the difference between passion and asthma. In short, telling "which kind of Oedipus Complex," would seem to me today to mean exploring more fully than I did yesterday these characteristic shifts, sequences, repetitions, re-creations, and new creations we commonly, and economically, refer to as oedipal conflicts and structures. In that sense, it would mean telling how a particular Oedipus complex both resembles and differs from all other Oedipus complexes.

I find that following my patients' and my self-inquiries seems to lead a bit more frequently than my earlier approaches to those extraordinary moments when there is revealed with more than usual clarity, and in near overwhelming complexity, the interpenetration of what we call past, present, and future. I find these to be the moments in which whatever I may say or otherwise do reverberates more clearly than usual on an extraordinary number of levels and in elaborately complex patterns within those levels. You know those moments— moments of opportunity—when, as a symphony, earlier phrases, themes, and movements return in new and unexpected unities and bear promise of still other possibilities.

Since, given how I work, these moments of amplification of one era within another seem most often and clearly to take place within an oedipal frame, and since these moments seem to provide heightened analytical opportunity for my patients and myself, I suppose it could fairly be said of my views of sexuality, neurosogenesis, analytical aims, and analytical mean that I'm a *latter-day* analytical oedipalist.

Trying to speak briefly, I've spoken too briefly. I want now to retrace a few steps.

I referred earlier to *amplifying oedipal* developments. In the analyses of those patients with whom I've worked— patients who cover the usual waterfront of characters and disorders—those amplifying oedipal developments are better characterized, I believe, as oedipal re-creations within adolescent re-creations. I believe that, as an analysis of an adult deepens, it more and more involves re-creations of adolescent psychological events. When things go best, current re-creations of adolescent re-creations of earlier events (especially of oedipal events and of preoedipal events that become oedipal) grow increasingly prominent. Simultaneously, re-creations of adolescent self-inquiries into those adolescent re-creations grow increasingly prominent.

I assume that the needs and capacities for self-inquiry take a quantum leap forward in adolescence and that one of the virtues of the free association method is that it invites what some have called "a second adolescence." By a second adolescence I mean not only a lively renewal of, and greater access to, the trials and tribulations of adolescence, and the trials and tribulations of the earlier eras re-created within adolescence, but a lively renewal of, and greater access to, the agendas and tools of inquiry of adolescence. I refer both to the tools that have since been sharpened and those that have since been dulled. (In some instances, in which original development seems to have taken a premature jump from childhood to adulthood, what we may see in analysis is in some respects a first adolescence.)

Those adolescent *turmoils and inquiries*—some conscious, most not, all highly sexual and aggressive—and the play of one with the other seem to me the raw material for much (I suspect most) creative and curative possibility. Or, to put it another way, I believe that what we commonly call regression in the service of the ego—we might call it regressive-progression—is often and perhaps usually a regression to the passions, turmoils, modes of inquiry, and thrusts toward development of adolescence.

To refer to regression to, or re-creation of, adolescent states is, of course, not to refer to exact repetitions. "We cannot walk in the same river twice." What I refer to, rather, are fluid yet cohesive ego states that resemble in many ways many states of adolescence. These states are marked especially by the intensity of antithetical and juxtaposed thrusts: thrusts toward forward development and thrusts toward blind repetition of the past.

I cannot here examine the interlocking chains of events observable in these adolescent re-creations. But I do want to stress that I'm not referring simply to an increase of conscious references to adolescent events (though there are sometimes some of those). I'm referring rather to such events as these:

a) shifts toward the language (the grammar, cadences, tones, accents, vocabulary, etc.) of that person's adolescence;

b) shifts toward adolescent gestures and postures;

c) frequent and brief expression of intense affects—often relatively untamed affects—alternating with frequent and brief mobilization of counteraffective measures;

d) frequent and rapid alternation of attitudes (for example, altruism and soloism, idealism and cynicism, hedonism and asceticism, romanticism and pragmatism);

e) prominent flux between integrative and disintegrative processes;

f) increasing preoccupation with body parts;

g) increasing interplay of early and late developmental configurations; and

h) increasing appearance of fragments of images, metaphors, and interests that in the person's actual adolescence served as materials for translating earlier experiences into ongoing experience and thus for translating fiction into fact and for unifying inner worlds and outer.

In short, I refer to analytical developments that, as in adolescence, make for the fullest possibilities for adaptive and maladaptive growth. These are the best of times and the worst of times. (I believe they are what Scott Fitzgerald called "moments of infinite possibility.")

I want to stress that I'm not saying that adolescent regression is by definition useful to analytical aims. Like anything else, it can in many ways serve the resistances. (Indeed, a clinging to adolescent developments can serve both to block access to earlier developments and to avoid movement to the future.) But I believe we more often see constructive adolescent-organized-and-organizing regression in the analytical situation, or something close to it, if, by our analytical personalities, tools, theoretical and other preferences, we do not encourage exclusive regressions to particular positions, adolescent or earlier.

I've found that if I follow the lead of my patients' self-inquiries as they emerge in their own good time, and if I help my patients to explore the confrontations between their inquiries and their self-imposed obstructions to those inquiries, I'm more likely to see these (ideal) adolescent regressions. I find that in this context patients—both those we commonly call neurotic and those we call "sicker"—reveal more clearly and can analyze more effectively the juxtapositions and interpenetrations of their intrapsychic conflicts *and* of their "primitive" arrests and defects. And in this context they seem to require somewhat fewer interventions beyond clarification and interpretation and even, on the average, to thrive on a diet of more clarifications and fewer interpretations.

There are, of course, always exceptions to such generalizations, and it would be folly to expect or insist that all patients proceed the same way. Exceptions abound in analytical work even if analytical proponents of one view or another rarely, if ever, propose adequate theories of exceptions. (And, even among patients who achieve the adolescent regressions of which I'm speaking, some take a bit longer than others.)

If it can be said that free association and other aspects of the analytical situation invite and advance a valuable adolescent regression in many patients, I think it can also be said that evenly hovering attention, and other aspects of the analytical situation, invite and advance a valuable adolescent regression in many analysts. (I don't say the regressions of patient and analyst are identical, only that they're in some ways similar.)

Allowing for differences between patients and analysts and among patients and among analysts, I think it can still be said that in the rekindling of the passions and the recovery of the tools of inquiry of adolescence lie many of the liveliest creative and curative possibilities for both the patient and the analyst. And, as in adolescence, many of those possibilities cannot become actualities unless common ground can be found for translating into mutually beneficial discoveries what were earlier for patient and the analyst largely solo analytical inquiries.

In short, I've come to believe that, on the average, analysis involves for both patient and analyst a reopening of inquiries and thrusts toward development of what I like to call the *curious adolescent:* curious by virtue of his or her turmoils, and curious about them.

The analyst's "adolescent regression" must be guided, of course, by good-enough psychoanalytical theory and knowledge. Few of us today would subscribe consciously to a naive romanticism that denies the importance of theory and knowledge nor to a naive pragmatism that imagines the possibility of a "pure" objectivity based on a linear application of our theory and knowledge. For most of us, the question is not whether we shall be guided by theory and knowledge (we accept that willy-nilly we always are) but by what theory and knowledge and in what fashion we shall be guided. Most of us, I believe, have learned and continue to learn that we can interfere in seemingly opposite ways with the disciplined improvisations necessary to the regressions in the service of the ego inherent in our method. One is wild analysis; the other is orthodoxy. (I say seemingly opposite ways because it could also be said these are both orthodoxies – old orthodoxies and fresh orthodoxies – and in both cases, as Erasmus might have put it, "Orthodoxy is the most successful apostasy.")

In struggling between the Scylla of wild analysis and the Charybdis of petrified analysis, the best aid we know, beyond the usual technical prescriptions for evaluating what we do, is persistent and ruthless self-inquiry, however limited that inevitably is. If self-inquiry is, as some persons say, so limited as to be useless, then I suspect there is no such thing as analysis, only applied analysis.

I suppose we would agree that some problems we face in achieving disciplined improvisation in our clinical work are kin to problems we face in achieving disciplined improvisation in our theory building. It seems to me therefore a probability – I suspect it's a certainty – that better clinical work will require not only a more adequate theory of neurosogenesis and of analytical aims and means, and not only that we develop a better taxonomy of disorder and better epigenetic schemes, but that we go farther in trying to temper our inclinations toward an undisciplined subjectivity and toward a spurious objectivity.

Which is also to say that we shall need to go farther in trying to attain a more persistently informed and examined subjectivity in our clinical work, in our theory building, and in the ways we link one to the other. And this will require, I imagine, that we build and employ an epistemology that more fully examines and embraces the disciplined subjectivity that comes of carefully learning, carefully "forgetting," carefully recovering, and carefully transcending our knowledge and theories.

AFTERTHOUGHTS

This previously unpublished paper was part of a panel discussion at a meeting of the American Psychoanalytic Association, Chicago, May 1987 (Gardner, 1987). We had been asked to tell how our views of sexuality and neurosogenesis had changed over the years and how those changes of view had changed how we practiced analysis.

Looking back, it seems clearer now than it did then that I was not simply doing what we had been asked. Though I would readily have concurred with the view that we never hear "simply" what we are asked, and we never respond "simply" to what we have heard, I seem to remember that I did think I was "simply" telling what I had been asked: how my views and practices had changed. Now, however, determined for the purposes at hand to look for "what else?" I find that I was both addressing the agenda at hand and simultaneously pursuing another. And perhaps the agenda at hand was secondary, and the "another" was primary. It seems to me now that the livelier agenda for me then was a reflection of my longstanding preoccupation with the nature of the analyzing instrument.

I don't like the term "instrument." It seems too mechanical. And I don't like the common usage that makes it the analyst's instrument, rather than, as Isakower intended, an overlap and interplay of the exploratory activities of patient and analyst. Still, the term is entrenched, and I bow to the entrenchment because I cannot think of a satisfactory way to name with one word these fluid events. Our language for describing mutualities—especially, though not only, mutualities of exploration—is as oddly impoverished in the analytic vocabulary as in others.

In any event, it seems to me now that my preoccupation and hidden questions about the nature of the analyzing instrument—and, for the purposes of the panel, the analyst's contribution—surfaced willy-nilly at the outset in my comments about learning French (shades again of Cher Pierre), and then more directly, if still tangentially, in my subsequent expression of the opinion that the main change in my analytic approach was that I no longer proceeded in the linear fashion from theory to practice that seemed implicit in the question we had been asked. In this sense, these opening remarks expressed my old and continuing preoccupation with the nature of the analyzing instrument in general and, in particular, insofar as both free association and evenly hovering attention are concerned, my preoccupation with the mysterious differences between applying a set of constructs directly and using those constructs flexibly—relatively flexibly—in the service of exploration and improvisation. Which preoccupation included highly troublesome and increasingly frequent questions about the differences between useful parsimonies and "hardening of the categories." I think my concern for the problems of attaining and maintaining an exploratory stance in the face of increasing accumulations of information was stimulated by observation of my own dilemmas, the dilemmas of other practitioners of analysis, and the dilemmas of practitioners of other fields marked by accumulations of sizeable masses of more or less useful information. (Since solitary miseries are often too much to bear, it is never difficult to affirm that other persons face temptations and tendencies similar to one's own.)

The remainder of this paper, whatever else it addresses, appears never far removed from hidden preoccupations with my own (and others'?) temptations and tendencies to replace with stale application what began in a spirit of exploration. (I have in mind both the incentives to stale application that arise from specific countertransferential tensions and those incentives that arise from the frequent choice to stick to the tried and true rather than face the uncertainties of fresh discovery.) In reaction to such problems, much of this paper joins the assigned topic—Sexuality, Neurosis, and Analysis—with an unassigned sketch of an effort to find ways of analyzing that lessen (slightly) what I had come to regard, and still regard, these ceaseless personal (and perhaps general) contraexploratory occupational hazards.

Chapter Eight

THE ART OF PSYCHOANALYSIS
On Oscillation and Other Matters

More than 50 years ago, an analyst said:

There are doubtless some analysts who would like to substitute knowledge for experiences. . . . There are perhaps at least as many analysts who commit another equally serious error. They misuse the idea of the analyst's unconscious as the instrument of his perception so that they do hardly any work at all in analysis but just "float" in it, sit and merely "experience" things in such a way as to understand fragments of the unconscious processes of the patient and unselectively communicate them to him. Thus there is no *oscillation* (my underlining) from intuition to understanding and knowledge which alone makes it possible to arrange in a larger context the material which has been understood with the help of the analyst's unconscious.

You may recognize these as the words of Otto Fenichel (1941). I hope he can help us to tune to the polyphany of yesterday's voices, today's, and tomorrow's, and so to consider some aspects of the changing state of our art.

I imagine we would agree to the cogency of Fenichel's warning. An art that loses its head is a lost art; a science that loses its art, a fossil science. Inclined to think and feel in polar extremes—indeed, to think of thinking and feeling as polar extremes—we're always at risk of getting lost at the poles.

Fenichel asks how we manage, when we manage, not to get lost. He replies, "We oscillate."

His question seems richer than his reply.

In poesy, Shakespeare asks:

> Tell me where is fancy bred?
> Or in the heart or in the head?
> How begot, how nourished,
> Reply. Reply.
> [*Merchant of Venice*]

Three centuries later, in prose, though not prosaically, Wordsworth replies:

> Our continued influx of feelings is modified
> and directed by our thoughts, which are indeed
> the representatives of all our past feelings.
> [*Lyrical Ballads*]

Fenichel seems at risk of shutting Wordsworth from the conversation. Both may have *aimed* at unitary ends, but Wordsworth talks of endless expanding and reorganizing transformations—unending, transcending reunions—and Fenichel simply of oscillation. The question I want to raise for consideration today is, What in the world is oscillation?

In our time, in a poem for children, David McCord (1980) says:

> "I think about the elephant and flea,
> For somewhere in between them is me.
>
> Perhaps the flea is unaware of this:
> Perhaps I'm not what elephants would miss.

I don't know how the flea puts in his day;
I guess an elephant just likes to sway.

But there they are: one little one and one large,
And in between them only me in charge!

I think McCord is on the right track. I want to say that he
wants to say it's a basic tendency of our minds to think in
polarities, unending polarities, and to put ourselves in the
middle. We define one thing as this and another as that, and
ourselves between this and that. This is our tendency, our
blessing and our curse. Having painstakingly divided our
worlds into opposites, we struggle always in the tension
between one and the other, a tension compounded of the
nature of our experiences and of our idiosyncratic ways of
viewing those experiences. We define what we see, we see
what we see, in the shape of our antithetical inclinations. We
find ourselves between what we see as opposites; and we try to
be what we regard as being in charge of them and ourselves.
That's life.

Once I had a patient who was involved in the development
of the computer. Moved by compassion for my ignorance, and
by other motives, he told often of things to come: "One of these
days," he said, "we'll organize everything we know in yes's
and no's, we'll feed it into computers, and we'll do things in
minutes that now take months. And we'll do other things we
can't even dream of doing now." He talked week after week of
the many possibilities; we analyzed one thing and another.
Then, hearing a change in the wind, or at least a distant rustle,
I asked:

"What about the things that don't fall into yes's and no's?"

"So much the worse for them," he replied.

He laughed. I asked about the laugh. He said my question
was one he wanted to think about—some day. Soon after, I
asked another question. He did not answer "yes." Neither did
he answer, "no." He answered, "Yo."

I'll not report the transferential details and other grist for the
analytical mill but, rather, suggest that this dialogue between
my patient and me is one we all hold sometimes with someone

else, more often with ourselves. We think binary; then we ask at last, "Well, what about the other?"

I think this dialogue, this effort to be in "charge" of imagined polarities, may be what Fenichel and others have called oscillation; if so, oscillation is like vacillation, only sturdier; if so, the difference between vacillation and oscillation is the difference between disorder and art. For brevity, I shall put questions as assertions.

In the practice of any art, we're always in argument with ourselves. Respectful argument. Not till the argument becomes too cranky or subdued are we in noticeable trouble: long indecison or hasty decision. When things go well, we make a virtue of our double vision; we see what we can see one way and then another, and sometimes, in ways hard to follow, both at once.

From the moment we first separate yes from no, we're polar thinkers. Forever after, we never stop making Arctics and Antarctics. Being, however, *both polar thinkers and something beyond,* we are, after all, not computers. At least, not yet. I read in the paper that some scientists predict that in five years it will be possible to build a brainlike computer with a web of connections of the complexity found in the brain . . . of a bee. I can believe that, but I cannot see how they will give the computer the right upbringing to think or act like a bee.

There's no sense in railing against binary thinking, dualistic, linear, Aristotelean, or related others, any more than against the spherical. We can't get by without the one *and* the other. We make one into two; we make two into one. East is East and West is West and always the twain shall meet. We imagine Yins and Yangs, concords and discords, Cinna the poet and Cinna the conspirator. In one mind, we demand to know which is which; in another, we couldn't care less. A McCord makes poles into poetry. An obsessional mocks polar thinking—and those he regards as its pushers—by mock deliberation. My computer patient used polar thinking for mathematics and mockery. As a child, he was already a master of the yo-yo. To his father who yelled at him to bring a glass of water, he yelled, "Hot or cold?"

The same pen writes the poetic and the picayune.

The mind cleaves. It cleaves in both senses of the old Anglo-Saxon word: it cuts apart, and it sticks to and together. In all our words and other thoughts we're committed dividers and addors, seekers of disparities and parities. Our endless hemmings and hawings, oppositions and unions, and other dialectical doings don't necessarily make us compulsion neurotic, or Hegelian, only human.

If such tumbling from thesis to antithesis to synthesis, and back, and forth, are oscillation, the term seems infelicitous. "Oscillation" is too leaden. Yet, cavorting may be too capricious. The mind in motion defies simple naming. In a New Yorker cartoon, the caption says, "We *lurch* to a different drummer."

Calling any elements of an art by their right names is hard. Perhaps impossible. But starting from the supposition that oscillation is shorthand for our protean efforts to play with the many polarities we inevitably and endlessly pose, I want to invite attention to some polarities (Fenichel names but a few), then to some related moves of the analyzing mind, and finally to some prospects for exploration and theory.

O f polar possibilities, there's never a shortage. Reconsider briefly the familiar plight of the first analyst.

In the beginning was affect. Affect, says Freud, is the main disordered and disordering force. Affect, when tied to unacceptable and banished idea, is blocked from direct and healthy expression and finds indirect and unhealthy expression. Cure lies in talk: talk leads to idea—the memory of traumatic, or otherwise unbearable event—which aids and abets expression of affect earlier finding egress only through tangential and troublesome means.

Occam himself might have been pleased by such elegant simplicity. Others might be pleased that this dovetailed theory of disorder, therapeutic aims, and therapeutic means seems, in principle, to promise equal attention to affect and idea. Some might surmise that such polar equality was Freud's conscious, almost conscious, or brewing intent.

Still, in the springtime of analysis, *affect* holds sway.

Idea, the idea Freud first takes to be memory, is merely the means to affective ends. If the laudable purging of affect were possible without remembrance of things past, Freud would not now consciously object (though, in some recess, we probably always object—exult and object—when we tear one world in two).

But soon, whether changes in his inner world lead those in his outer, or outer lead inner, or, more likely, with inner and outer in lively exchange, Freud makes the well-known discovery that turns his world and ours inside out. He finds wishful thinking in what he had earlier judged faithful recording. With that, stress shifts from affect to idea: shifts, that is, to wish and fantasy, which, even more than before, seems to promise a balanced vision: this time, affective idea or perhaps ideational affect. Besides, in rough parallel, in his coeval theory of the mind, he posits that drives and their derivatives—now our special concern—take form *both* in affect and in idea.

All that notwithstanding, from today's vantage point, Freud's case histories seem not to reflect a steady balance, either static or moving, between affect and idea, but rather, on balance, a professorial tip toward *idea*, with occasional contrapuntal moves between the one and the other.

It's a long way to heaven—if heaven is the union of affect and idea.

Nor need we believe in arrivals if we distinguish Freud 2 from Freud 3: distinguish the Freud who failed to see that where there was his smoke was Dora's fire from the Freud who begins to see the many shapes and shadows of transference.

Transference analysis makes room for fuller play between affect and idea, experiencing and understanding, past and present, inner and outer, fact and fiction, and other products of our patients' and our inclinations to construct polar worlds of elephants and fleas. But these halcyon moments of fructifying unification, amplification, and transformation, however wonderful, are not ever-lasting. (The halcyon, you may recall, was a mythical bird fabled to nest on the sea at the winter solstice and thereby, *briefly*, to calm the waves.)

No matter how worthy the unities, affective-ideational and other, that transference analysis makes possible, neither this nor any tool can long tame our urges to make poles of affect and idea. And of much else. Indeed, the same tools we use to advance unities, we are adept at using to overturn.

Could we do otherwise?

Of our dealings with another of our polarities—self and surround—a distinguished biologist once said, "I wonder what the world would be if we defined ourselves not as bounded by our skins but by that plus two feet beyond."

If things were different, they'd doubtless be different. Meanwhile, let us take them as we ordinarily make them.

If we regard Freud's struggles to unite affect and idea neither as struggles of beginner, or genius, or other particular sort, nor as struggles ended once and for all for him, or us, they become a mirror of our own. Viewed so, they reflect our unending constructions, deconstructions, and reconstructions of warring dualities and transient pacific unities. Viewed so, his struggles are not a relic of our past, nor his solutions something we simply and safely inherit. They are spur to our self-inquiries. I want to mention that now and come back to it soon.

If I invite you to review some differences in how analysts possess their poles, I hope you won't think I do so to toast or roast our diversity. Rather, I mean to highlight some aspects of that diversity for ends I hope to make clear.

What I shall say of analysts at large comes in good part from extended exchanges with 48 captive analysts in what is sometimes known by that unfortunate term "super-vision." The shortest has spanned three years, the longest, ten. Thirty-six have been with analysts who would generally be regarded inexperienced; twelve, experienced.

Other impressions come from self-observation and from those many episodic observations of colleagues here and abroad that are the lot of any analyst who hangs out where many hang out. In the respects I shall try to outline, the most experienced were not conspicuously different from the least; most did what the least did, though often less transparently.

When I was a boy there was a comic strip called "Reglar Fellers." Each time, some ragamuffins would play happily in the streets, and each time, one of them would say, with obvious self-content, "I wonder what the poor kids are doing today?" You may think the ways I shall sketch are the ways of poor analysts. Problematic approaches to one set of poles or another do seem the mark of some analysts in particular, and of some groups, but I want to invite attention to ways in which polar play may be the mark of all.

Most analysts seem intent on advancing unities of affect and idea, but few seem to go at it the same way. They use different palettes. They mix their colors in different proportions.

Some analysts seem to prefer affects that many would regard as pale. They seek the pale either by less attention to transference or by more. In the latter case, they arrange for a muting of affects by the predictability of their attention to transference (or defense, or other particular) or by the relative uniformity of their means of attending. To some analysts, those analysts would seem specialists in the use of rituals that calm.

Others welcome what some would regard as affect storms. Thunderous storms. They seem eager to bail out oceans with sieves; to some analysts, they would seem specialists in rituals that excite. (To make matters more complicated, some analysts would say of some who seem to seek strong affect that they seek not affect but sentimentality.)

Some analysts prize what others would regard as intellectualizing, and others prize what some would regard as affectualizing; what some regard as just the right blend of heart and head, others regard as obstructive understatement or obstructive hyperbole: defensive, defective, or both.

Beauty here, as elsewhere, is in the eye of the beholder.

What's more, what calms some analysts excites others; what excites some calms others. Some analysts work better in conditions of calm, and others, excitement. Some are calmed by exciting others. Some are excited by calming others. Some prefer to be more awake; some favor dreamier states.

Designating some things transference and some not—making poles, that is, of transference to ourselves and transference to others (a juxtaposition not without gain for some ends)—we wonder sometimes if we should now attend more carefully to what our patients regard as else or to what we regard as us. Having put ourselves in that middle, we sometimes ask more about else, sometimes, "What about me?" Some seem more apt to opt for other, some for me.

Making poles of accuracy and confusion, some track transference more avidly for confusion: how and why a patient is now confusing past and present. Others are more alert to accurate evocations: how the past has sharpened acuities for like happenings in the present. All analysts I have seen have an eye for each but, I've never seen one with equal eyes. All things being unequal, some are more adept at finding their patients' understandings; others, misunderstandings.

One finding may lead to the other—and usually does—but never the same way and never with the same accents.

Take another design. Making poles of past and present, we're bound sometimes to wonder whether it would be better to regard the past as figure and present as ground, or present as figure and past as ground. Most analysts try to follow the affective lead of their patients—and to follow other pole stars—but it is easy to see that one analyst steps a bit more briskly to the tunes of the here-and-now, and another to the there-and-then. (We all know analysts who dash to the one or the other, but I am referring here to more ordinary and gentler differences of steppage.) I've found no analyst I could describe as equidistant or in a steady swing, even syncopated swing, between history and current event. One seems a bit partial to modern construction, another to antique reconstruction. And each shows many partialities within the one and the other.

Even when we see what we regard as the past emerging in what we regard present, we do not all do so the same way. One sees blind repetition a shade more easily, another the thrust toward development. (We know that nothing is all one or the other, but I am talking of what we do, not what we know.)

And when we picture what "must" have taken place in the past or "must" be taking place in the present, some are more inclined to regard their pictures as photographs—old-fashioned, objective photographs—some as impressionist paintings. Making poles of objective and subjective, of real and imagined, of literal and metaphorical, one opts a trifle more avidly for the one, another for the other. One is, on the whole, earthier, another, ethereal. Nor are these preferences always what they at first seem; one asks for "fact" when seeking "fiction," another for "fiction" when seeking "fact."

Making poles of speech and silence, some are quicker to speak, some slower. Picasso was fond of the old painter's adage: "Of any subject, destroy your first painting. Better still, destroy the second and third; the one you paint at last will be shaped by the others and be better for it." Other painters prefer the voices that say: "Strike while the iron is hot!" Shall we say that a hot-blooded fellow like Picasso should foreswear a hard-won fondness for the return engagement? for delayed interpretation? his resolve to be fond? Art demands one thing of one of us, something else of another. Some analysts are more like Picasso, others seem anti-Picasso. It seems better if we are what we are, but not always. It seems likely that Picasso was not always Picasso, not always like what he thinks, or says, is Picasso.

Quick or slow on the draw, some analysts see interpretation more as staple, others less. Some tend to regard patients as needing an interpretation; others tend to regard patients as needing to find out what makes it seem they need an interpretation. Some analysts stress what they know, some what they don't.

Polarities compound polarities. Some stress the benefits of insight, some the expansion of abilities for insight, some what goes on between patient and analyst in trying to expand the one or the other. All analysts are involved in each, but never equally.

I don't want to forget the poles we often make of questions

and answers. Some analysts regard questions as intrusive. Others regard statements as intrusive. Some are especially good at asking questions that are statements, others at making statements that are questions.

I suppose it might go without saying, but let's say it: among analysts who seem by and large to share the same visions of analysis, some are slightly bigger on the oedipal, others on the pre, some on finding where one meets the other. Some zoom in more quickly on conflict, some on defect. And within the one context or the other, one is more sensitive to nuances of body image, another to other conceptions of self, another to the self in connection with other persons, and another to other connections with the animate or inanimate world.

Some tune more alertly to how patients victimize themselves, some to how patients have been victimized by others. (We all seem to know there's guilt enough for all; but I'm still talking of what we do, not what we know.)

One goes for defense with a vengeance; another is a bit quicker on what's defended against. Of those who attend most to defense, some attend one way, some another.

Some seem better informed by the empathy of soothe and some by the empathy of challenge; indeed, some seem to regard empathy as nothing but the right way to agree, others as nothing but the right way to disagree. Which is to say, some are more inclined to be agreeable, some disagreeable.

One analyst accents bellicose intentions; another, the tensions of love. One is most attentive to the dreams dreamed asleep, another to dreams dreamed awake. One is more finely tuned to the content of tales told, another to how told, and still another to what the teller perceives as the analyst's response to what's told. Good-enough analysts are attuned to all, but each a trifle more to one or the other.

Some analysts can barely contain themselves at the sound, sight, or other sense of a continuity; others of a discontinuity. Some, that is, show a sharper vision for fits, others for misfits. Over time, each seems to go from one to the other and sometimes to combine the one and the other, but, here too, no two the same way. Every perception, like every other interpretation, tells at least as much about the perceiver as about the perceived.

I am not now speaking of blind spots, countertransference, or other problems, but of different aptitudes and propensities. I have found no analysts who handle their poles with even-handed dexterity. And they are even more their idiosyncratic selves in the ways they discover and implement what in principle they knew all along: that they need not in the first place have made their poles so separate. The specifics of their synthesizing and transcending moves are always a surprise and arrived at by twists and turns whose eccentricity never has struck me as having the predictability of oscillation.

When I was starting out in analysis, my first two supervisors, whom I saw back to back, puzzled me. One spoke as if she relied only on intuition. The other spoke as if he consciously figured everything out with precise and elaborate logic. It was a relief to learn, at last, that each smuggled in the currency of the other. Some analysts accent empathy, some intuition, some a more conscious logic. In our enthusiasm for one way, especially for talking of one way, we often blur the importance of what we smuggle, how we smuggle, when we smuggle, and how we mix the one bounty with the other. Of all the arts that make up our art, smuggling is probably tops. If I may be permitted an avuncular note: trust no analysts who deny they smuggle!

We know these differences among analysts; privately, we sometimes take some into account. But in our theory building we seem largely to ignore our differences—and what difference they make—unless they are large enough to divide us into camps. What is more, and it probably counts more, we seem content to ignore the ways we differ not merely from each other but from ourselves.

Tolstoy remarks that we say one person is like this and another like that as if both are always the same. He reminds us that people are, to the contrary, like rivers; they run shallow in some parts, deep in others, fast here and slow there, warm here and cold there.

I see no reason to exempt analysts. Only over time do we

achieve what on balance might be regarded balance. In the analyzing mind, as in other minds, as in most animate and inanimate affairs, balance is the long addition of short imbalances, especially of imbalances viewed from afar. Though I've found few analysts who seem wild swingers, neither have I found any who occupy a post between their poles in what I regard middle of the road. Nor have I ever seen persistently balanced swings between the extremes of an arc; I suspect such mechanical constancies may be a purgatory in which we're better off not. (I have observed in myself and others brief steady swings between one pole and another, but these have special purposes and cannot, I think, be regarded our usual itineraries.)

The more I think about oscillation, the stranger it sounds to my mind's ear. Fans oscillate. Machines oscillate. Parts of machines oscillate. I don't know how I could have believed that analysts oscillate.

When things go well enough, our movements are considerably friskier. We are not every day, every hour, or every moment all one way or the other. We move most quickly and most often where we move best, though moving well enough and often enough where we move less well. We can be relied on not to be long at one of our poles, nor in one place between, nor in the same voyage between the one and the other. (We can especially be relied on to be moving and movable because most analyses can be relied on to be long.) When things go well enough, we have, like one of Kafka's characters, "no fixed abode."

In the pursuit of our art, we arrange and rearrange endlessly those particular stances and movements we prefer and need for carrying out our ever-changing analyzing aims and our ever-changing other aims and the necessary blending of the two. By other aims, I refer to aims responsive to extraanalytic events of our lives, changes of mood, and changes in our physical condition, and to those other changing challenges, satisfactions and dissatisfactions, and flashes of health and madness that make up our everyday lives.

Neither wild nor static nor in pendular swing, the analyzing mind in motion—a restless mind—follows a tortuous path. When things go well enough, we meander, wander, leap, lurch, trip, and otherwise move from one state to another and, occasionally, to a united state.

These various motions of the analyzing mind, in trouble or not, shape persistently the unfolding of each analysis. A "spontaneous" unfolding of analytic happenings— an unfolding relatively free of the influence of the analyst's ways of moving between his or her self-appointed poles—seems about as frequent as spontaneous generation.

Our polar preferences—our preferred means of moving from one pole to the other, our preferred means of going beyond the limits of our poles, the virtues and defects of our preferences, and our ways of managing those virtues and defects—all warrant, I believe, thorough observation, which means largely self-observation and, occasional self-observation assisted by our consultants.

If there is value in regarding the analyst a constant—a relative constant—and the patient a constant variable, I imagine we could agree there is value in sometimes considering things the other way round. It may be understandable that for simplicity, in the early growth of our field, we spoke of the analyst mainly as constant—whether in fixed position or in the constancy of swings—and, though admitting to occasional variations that come of occasional disturbances, paid scant attention to other and more constant variations.

It would be unfortunate, however, if, in holding to these sometimes useful fictions, we obscured the workings of our art in a cloak of imagined uniformity. Still, it's one thing to concede that we differ from each other and from ourselves, and another to explore, day in and day out, our *constancies and fluidities and their impact on the particulars of the analyses we conduct*.

We may dare to do it or not, but map carefully, over time, one analyst's moves from one pole to another and we've mapped that analyst's theory, method, and character.

To survive and thrive, any art and any science must become an art-science. But what is the nature of the hyphen?

The hyphen, I believe, is, by necessity and choice, polar play. We try to move between the poles we call, and therefore make, art and science. We try to be guided by experience and theory; we try not to confine our vision to what we consequently expect. In analysis, what comes in handy for our double aim—what comprises the hyphen that separates and joins art and science and other self-made poles—is free attention. (To "freely floating" or "evenly hovering,"or "evenly suspended," I prefer "free" attention for its hint of likeness to free association. Besides, when we free attend, there's not much about it that strikes me as even, floating, suspended or hovering.)

The free-attending mind is like other minds, only more so. In free attention, our polar sporting—our habit of setting up poles and trying to make the best of the habit—is given freer play. If polar play finds room in all thought, it finds fuller province in free attention.

There, we are mainly minding our p's' and q's. We cannot think of anything—call it p—without contrasting it with its opposite—call it q. Our poles once set, we try to take "charge" of that setting. Now we seek differences and distinctions. Now, we use contrast to highlight likeness. Now we find p; now we find q; now we see p as q in reverse. And now, when we can, we make p and q figures in a larger alphabet.

We take alphabets apart to use our letters separately. We take alphabets apart to rebuild them: nothing being long holdable except by the endless, ongoing demolition and rebuilding we call "structure." We take alphabets apart to make new. Relatively new. We go forth to go back, and back to go forth. And, finding it easier to ignore differences when we don't know the difference, we go back to the days when we knew no differences; we go back from the polar to the prepolar, and we play between confusion and integrative creation.

We take things apart; we put them together. Having put them together, we cannot wait to take them apart. Where our polar play is most lively lie the largest possibilities for learning and discovery.

Each art-science has its characteristic poles and its characteristic tools for seeking the disciplined fluidity of polar play. Our tool is free attention. As an analysis proceeds, if things go well, that play becomes faster and more fluid. Where rule fails, hunch helps; where hunch fails, rule helps. When things go best, rule helps hunch helps rule. When free attention holds sway, there's no quibble between intuition and knowledge, thinking and feeling, words and vision, inner and outer, past and present, and our other ways of sensing and making sense. And when things go best, a quickening of these moves of the free attending mind meets and is met by synchronous quickenings in our free-associating patient.

What saves us, then, when we are saveable, from both our readiness to endorse sessile positions and our wild swings— neither of these finding new angles of vision—are the unending corrections and countercorrections that come of our moves, in free attention, between and beyond the poles we arrange within and around our selected and evolving experience. When things go best, we maintain a moving and originative inconsistency even when claiming to adhere to formulaic and static concepts. But when we surrender free attention, and its enhanced polar play, for direct application of our experience and our theory, we risk trading symphonies for single notes.

In the practice of our art, as in any art, we need room for habit and room for whim. Flexible habit and informed whim. If the analyzing mind ranges more widely and fluidly than our chronicles suggest, I suppose that should be no surprise. Scientists now tell us that not even a pendulum's path is as straight or simple as we earlier imagined. Apparently we need a science of order and a science of chaos.

Yet, if we did no more than wobble, ramble, amble, lurch, leap, and otherwise move between our self-appointed poles, we'd be well on our way to confusing freedom with license. The free attending mind does not oppose guiding generalizations of experience and theory, only naive faith in guiding generalizations. Neither does it replace naive faith with nihilism, nor commit us to a Luddite fear of theory's frames. Free attention helps us to take theory and experience in that spirit Kenneth Clarke imagined must have gone into the building of Gothic cathedrals: a spirit of serious play.

Analysts have spent much time – sometimes well – weighing the advantages of one or another theory of disorder and of therapeutic aims and means. We've applied the well-known criteria of consistency, truth, and heuristic value. We've shaped our clinical theories with regard to the disorders and strengths of the patients we hope to help.

But we have devoted less attention to shaping our theories with regard for the free-attending workings of the minds that will use those theories. Improving our theories for some purposes, we do not necessarily improve them for the use of the analyzing mind. Nor does the theory that best serves one analyzing mind necessarily best serve another.

Which theories, current or impending, might best serve the workings of the average analyzing mind is not our topic today, nor do I think it could be tomorrow or the day after. I believe we need to observe those workings more carefully before we can well address that question. Meanwhile, we might do well neither to argue too fiercely the virtues of one theory over another, nor to settle our differences prematurely by making our theory an Esperanto. Universal, eclectic, and ecumenical visions may be good for peaceable kingdoms, high-level discussions, and other slumber parties, but exploratory travel needs the momentum of bursts of disciplined short-sightedness.

Our free attention is not what it was yesterday, nor will it be tomorrow what it is today. Free attention moves moment to moment between, and occasionally beyond, all the poles we can now imagine and are learning to imagine.

Free attention is advanced and constrained by what the free attendor preconceives and otherwise prefigures, which is advanced and constrained both by evolving theory and experience and by the personal inquiries necessary to the free attendor's own growth. All is lit by the light of our dawning needs. In our simplest perception, need plays its part: a tree is not the same when we're looking for firewood as for shade.

And when need embraces needs of self and other, complexity compounds complexity. We see what we need most to see, and, when things go well enough, what we need most to see is shaped by a sense of possibility for self and other, an informed self-centeredness. When things go well enough, free attention makes it a bit easier to maintain a foolish consistency in our analytical precepts than in our analytical percepts and other acts. Which perhaps may be a piece of what we have meant right along in praise of "oscillation."

Some years ago a sign outside a London club read: "Dogs are not permitted on the premises." Below had been added another sign: "Any dog leading a blind person shall be deemed a cat."

All clubs have such signs. Our club is no exception. We patch old visions long after we know they require fuller revision. We have a sign that says: "Do Not Disturb! Oscillators and mirrors at work; they attend evenly, neutrally, and anonymously, with equidistance from all known poles." We have signs that patch these, signs too long and many. Our signs say some things worth saying, but not quite what we mean.

Some critics might say that our signs show traces of a comfortable and comforting myth of the unencumbered observer, a fin de siecle myth – 19th not 20th – a myth of the detached purity of the scientific mind. Perhaps so. With what we analysts have observed over almost a century, we have much to be pleased; with what we know of how we observe, less.

We have many possibilities of observing how we observe. Why do we know so few? Some might say our ignorance is willful: to observe how we observe is not impossible, only painful. We often watch the countertransference with admirable care. But, having performed that praiseworthy task, we act as if we have explored all that needs exploring; indeed we use our attention to countertransference to support the myth that our observations are otherwise pure. Or relatively pure.

The scientist might ask, how can you fail, nowadays, to examine more throroughly how your position influences what you observe? The art buff might ask, when painters have long shown that red seen with green is not the same as red alone, how can you fail to look more carefully at your arrangements of reds and greens? The epistemologist might ask, how can you, in the age of relativity, fail to apply more of relativity's visions to your analyzing vision? All might ask, how can you, who explore the unrecognized in yourselves and others, pay such small heed to the horizons—the sensitivities, outlooks, interests, philosophies, ethics and other organizers—that prescribe what and how you explore?

All might warn: in trying to assert that you're not wild, take care not to assert that you're inert.

Though I think these critics a bit harsh, I cannot, in the main, disagree. I think we do cling to old myths of "immaculate perception." Failing to pay more attention to how we pay attention, we have failed to learn much we might of what hampers our free attention and what enhances. Not knowing our art, we risk losing it. We might concede that.

Yet, we have begun, I think, to rewrite old signs. Last spring in Montreal, Weinshel (1990) suggests that we may be entering an era of increasing modesty. That may include a slight tempering of our claims to purity of vision and, with it, perhaps, the bitter-sweet pleasure of knowing more what we are doing. We have begun the job of juxtaposing visions of the normally balanced analyst with visions of the normally unbalanced. That takes time. Some day, we shall put both poles on our signs, and someday, new unities of the two.

Through long preparation for self-observation, we have a chance to observe more fully the workings of the analyzing mind, to develop new theories and new models of those workings—linear and spiral—and to develop a language that moves more flowingly between art and science, a bilingualism of form and vocabulary in both our reports and our theories. Sticking too much to the one language or the other, we censor much that fails to fit. The hyphen between art and science must be addressed by polar play. It takes a hyphen to catch a hyphen.

Through fuller self-observation of the analyzing mind in motion, we have a chance to learn more of our art and so of other arts. And, learning more of these arts, we have a chance to learn more of perception, representation, recall, and other creativities of the mind in its everyday artful preoccupations.

AFTERTHOUGHTS

This essay was presented as a plenary address to the American Psychoanalytic Association, San Francisco, May, 1989. It was later published in the *Journal of the American Psychoanalytic Association* (Gardner, 1991a).

"Art," returning to my preoccupation with "evenly hovering attention," begins with and takes off from Fenichel's notion of "oscillation." On starting out as an analyst, I was impressed by Fenichel's characterization of the analyzing mind not so much as "hovering" but rather as a mind in motion. "Oscillation" struck me as reflecting his intention to stress the importance of shifts from one perspective to another. Later, however, I began to wonder about his characterization of that motion as "oscillation." Still later, I became quarrelsome. Having at first been impressed by Fenichel's stress on mobility, I began to quarrel with what I took to be the mechanical connotations of "oscillation."

That quarrel may not have been entirely fair. Mechanical models of the mind—of the analytical mind or other—clearly have their virtues. They intend to simplify; and they do. Still, "oscillation," like "analyzing instrument" and other of our entrenched analogies, does not help us to ponder—and perhaps helps us to obscure—the fluidity of the events in question.

My quarrel was not solely with what I took to be—and still take to be—the implication of mechanical regularity in "oscillation." It was also, and especially, with the implication of mechanical perfection (shades of "immaculate perception"). Though I could appreciate Fenichel's effort to warn against one-sided approaches—single-strandism being one of the most prominent forms of apostasy throughout the history of psycho-analysis—I was not tickled by the implied separation of a cadre of analysts who oscillate and a lesser breed who fail to.

I found it more congenial to imagine—and my observations of myself and others had reinforced the preference to imagine—that the analyzing mind in motion was, for good and for bad, not so steady as Fenichel imagined. As a consequence of these observations and speculations, I tried to preserve his notion of motion but to characterize the motion differently. It was in that mix of appreciation and dissension that I tried in this paper to underscore a basic custom of all human animals, including the analytical, to perceive and conceive of their experiences in polarities; and it seemed to me therefore their inescapable fate to struggle ever after to make the best of their custom of perceiving and conceiving in polarities.

In that context, I tried to suggest that in analyzing, as in pursuit of other (relatively) creative activities, we may manage occasionally to move irregularly—to lurch and the like—between one of our constructed poles and another, but rarely if ever do we manage to "oscillate." Accordingly, I offered the view that, although we sometimes manage some sorts of motion and sometimes even arrive at (make) some sorts of unities where before we saw only disparities, we do not move constantly or evenly between the happenings Fenichel re-marked upon nor between the many other happenings we experience as antithetical. Inevitably, we perambulate un-evenly. And, equally inevitably (Is there such a thing as unequally inevitably?), and perhaps more frequently, we halt. And when we halt, we occupy positions—characteristic tilts—at, or nearer, one pole or the other. Which is why "We're always at risk of getting lost at the poles." All of us.

It was from this vantage point that I offered the opinion that if it is true, as I imagine it to be, that all of us are polar thinkers—some more conspicuously and others less— and all move irreg-ularly and all sometimes get stuck at, or nearer to, one of many poles, it might be useful to try persistently to explore the nature and the consequences of our frequent departures from our ideals of hovering, oscillating, or otherwise maintaining a mind in motion. (Though I was unaware of it in the writing, this stress on the inevitability of frequent departures from our analyzing ideals returns to and elaborates, I believe, on my earlier discussion of Spruiell's paper in chapter 2.)

A friend who was present when I presented this paper told me that after my presentation, he went to the men's room. There he observed one man standing next to another and he overheard the one man say to another, "This stuff was just a rehash of what they covered in my college course in philosophy." Which I suppose goes to show how risky it is for an analyst to have—or propose—any commerce with philosphy and philosophers.

Chapter Nine

AND WHO WILL ANALYZE
THE ANALYSTS?

D o you remember what Winnie-the-Pooh said of his spelling?

"It's good spelling," he said, "But it wobbles and the letters get in the wrong places."

I find the same of my self-analysis. It's good analysis, but it wobbles and the letters get in the wrong places.

I've come to regard self-analysis as one of those noble human endeavors that ranks considerably higher in desireability than possibility. Sometimes self-analysis seems an endless exercise in one hand clapping, an elaborate self-deception, a thinly disguised hypochondriasis. Sometimes the very notion of self-analysis seems oxymoronic. And sometimes I can't help but agree with those who say there's no such thing as self-analysis.

And yet I've come also to believe that without that no such thing, there's no such thing as psychoanalysis. Most of what I am saying here will be variation on that paradox of necessity

122

and impossibility. Much will invite too much attention to my own experience; but of so autobiographical a venture as self-analysis I know little except the autobiographical, and too little of that.

With the term self-analysis I'm discontent. I find it well suited to evoke fruitless comparisons and contrasts—invidious distinctions—between activities we call self-analysis and those we call psychoanalysis. Therefore, I want to say right off:

I don't believe one person alone can do all that two together can do. I don't believe two together can do all that one alone can do. I don't believe self-analysis can replace psychoanalysis or psychoanalysis can replace self-analysis. I regard two heads as better than one for some purposes and one better than two for some purposes. I believe that, however much the joy of polemics might sometimes invite us to pit self-analysis and psychoanalysis, ideally, they serve each other in unending, if unsteady, reciprocity.

To separate the solo activity from the two-party, and to pave the way for occasional rapprochement, I prefer the term self-inquiry to self-analysis. By self-inquiry I refer especially to those inquiries for which, through our experiences on and behind the couch, and through other peculiarities of opportunity and temperament, analysts seem especially prepared (or to which especially attracted): inquiries that shape and are shaped by events in the twilight between the more awake and the more dreamlike.

But I'm getting ahead of myself. When I was starting out as an analyst, my inquiries were of a different ilk and unfolded in a different light. I paid particular attention to matters to which my analyst and I had earlier paid particular attention. I asked myself questions he'd asked or I imagined he might ask; I commented in ways he'd commented or I imagined he might comment. In the main, these inquiries served as footnotes to my analysis and sometimes, in favorable instances, as workings-through.

As I look back at those first postanalytical efforts—at least, those I set down in my journals—many seem harmless and some, useful, but many are hampered by my consistency in rounding up the usual suspects. Over and over, exploration of the known seems to have helped me to take fuller possession of that ground and to avoid the rigors of exploring as yet unexplored and bumpier terrain. Over and over, at the cross-roads between the old and the new, I seem to have opted resolutely for the old.

Obvious as it seems that the road-taken fails to take the taker on the road-not-taken, still, whenever I inquire into yesterday's inquiries, I'm startled to find the many mind-closing conse-quences and the mind-closing purposes of yesterday's mind-openers. I'm troubled to see how often my cleaving to the familiar was aided and abetted by clear manifestations of the Jack Horner syndrome. (You remember that young Horner put his thumb in the pudding, pulled out a plum and said, "What a good boy am I.") Self-plumbing and self-patting seem inex-tricably bound.

Reexamining my early postanalytic inquiries and, not infre-quently, subsequent inquiries, I've found myself too often too sanguine about the value of continuing what I learned in my analysis and too skeptical that either my agendas or means of inquiry could profitably be expanded. So much for cleaving too much to my analysis. I also find problems of cleaving too little: of ignoring, that is, the dearth of regression-inviting and the plethora of regression-inhibiting circumstances in my self-inquiries in contrast to analysis. Which is to say, I've too often ignored the problems of being both analyst and analysand. It's one thing to manage a useful regression in the presence of a helpful other; it's another to manage it alone.

I think I assumed at the outset that efforts to explore my dreams—telling my dreams to myself and associating to them as I'd earlier told them to my analyst and myself and associated to them—would automatically ease me into one of those dreamy but self-observant states essential for other than cur-sory self-inquiry. Looking back, however, it seems to me that though contemplating my dreams sometimes did make me desirably dreamful, it often made me too wakeful. (I might even say fretful.) Moreover, I seem too often to have moved too easily to plausible explanations that opened few unexpected vistas. Too many words, too little music.

In short, dreams may have proved a royal road for Freud's self-inquiries, but my dreams led me—or I led them—all too often in all too familiar circles. In retrospect, I realize there was no good reason to assume that what worked well enough for Freud in his self-inquiries—well enough in some ways—and what worked well enough in my own analysis—well enough in some ways—would necessarily work well enough in my self-inquiries. In saying this, I don't mean to demean dream analysis, still less to recommend how others should inquire, but rather to observe that I've found it necessary to search repeatedly for fresh ways of achieving conditions helpful to self-inquiry. If I persist too long in a familiar way, dream inquiry or other, I find it brings me mainly familar news.

In persisting, nevertheless, at the start—and too often since—in ways that proved useful but not too useful, I've often, probably always, proceeded at cross purposes: trying both to advance inquiry and to avoid both the necessary regressions and the impulses, affects, and insights to which those regressions might have led. I doubt it will surprise you to hear that I've found that the deficiencies of my inquiries have not simply been the consequence of inevitable selective inattention—that, looking at the familiar, I could not look at the unfamiliar—nor of my frequent overburdening of self-inquiry with the task of tempering the distresses of analytic and other separation, nor of my persistent failure to grasp the need for a well-tempered regression. I've found the deficiencies of my inquiries to be willful exploitations of these and other inquiry-constricting possibilities. Which is to say, I've found what one might expect I'd have known all along—and in some ways did, but in others did not—that every method I choose for advancing my inquiries has the defects of its virtues; and every method is chosen both for those virtues and those defects.

Whenever I inquire into my inquiries, those long past or current, I find signs that I wanted and tried to limit the very inquiries I thought I was most avidly and single-mindedly pursuing. I find my inquiries always in the tension between my inclinations to advance and my inclinations to retard them. I would not dare mention such an obvious finding, except it's one thing to be acquainted with that tension in principle, it's another to find a way to explore its particulars.

My inquiries into the nature of my inquiries, and later into the self-imposed obstacles, began largely as byproducts of other efforts or, perhaps, of my finding something I was looking for without being aware I was looking. They began – or at least began to come to my attention – some 20 or so years ago when I set out to learn more about what went on in me while analyzing my patients. I've tried elsewhere to describe those efforts, and I want now simply to restate and expand a few pieces.

Looking at my analyzing efforts over a dozen or more years, I began to realize how often during analytic hours I was seeing things: seeing visual images, ephemeral visual images, of which I'd earlier been unaware. And when, after analytic hours, I associated to the details of those in-hour images, as one might to a dream, I was startled to find how much was revealed of my inner worlds, of my patients' inner worlds, and of ways in which the two inner worlds became shared outer worlds.

At first, I assumed that such two-faced tachistoscopic images unfolded in similar ways and, for similar purposes, in all analysts. I suspect that this assumption, whether partly correct or not, served my defensive eagerness to disavow the oddities of my own experience, the conflicted unconscious purposes, and the dawning awareness that I'd come upon a way of advancing my inquiries that promised to be exceedingly unsettling. I know I was uneasy about confessing to the ubiquitous presence of the very images whose presence in an analyst's head not a few analysts regarded as sure signs of the invasion of primary process and of the breakdown – actual or impending – of analytical functioning. (Such a scunner against the visual may seem odd nowadays, but in those days, I believe it was more common.)

In any case, I still think that visual images play a special and insufficiently explored role in the analyzing inlook and outlook of many, perhaps all, analysts, a role often obscured by our long-established habits of replacing image worship with word worship. (I take some comfort from the similar views of Isakauer, Lewin, Malcove, and others.) And I still believe—I like to believe—that thinking in images instead of words or, rather, moving rapidly back and forth between the image and the word—a very ancient travel—makes possible (when possible) enlightening play on the chiaroscuro border between creative discovery and trouble.

But, even if seeing things in evanescent hieroglyphs is widespread and even if most analysts employ many different tools of perception and representation, each relies especially, I now admit, on preferred edge-of-awareness experiences derived from preferred senses and mixes of senses. Which has led me to the view that insofar as our preferences—chosen and imposed—present different possibilities for self-inquiry and different openings to our inner worlds, we might be said to have different holes in our heads.

I would like to know a bit more about how things go, or might go, for those who, when proceeding most characteristically, are seers, hearers, proprioceptive reactors, gut reactors, and other actors. In an effort to invite such ecumenical sharing of idiosyncrasy, I offer the following example, one that moves between the analysis of a patient and my own self-inquiry. In passing, I'll mention a few things about self-observation and self-inquiry and shall leave the other piece of the triptychal subject of this panel, reanalysis, to others.

One day, in an analytic hour, I saw the image of a dozen or so irregularly shaped pieces of wood scatterd on a table. That evening, I recalled the image and wondered if the pieces of wood might be pieces of a puzzle. I rejected the notion on the grounds that it did not look like a puzzle. At which, I suddenly thought: "Oh. That's it. It's a puzzle that doesn't look like a puzzle."

I suspected that my image contained a useful reference to events of the analytic hour in which it had been formed but I had no idea—no conscious idea—what the reference might be.

Nor could I recall at what point in the hour I'd seen the image of the puzzle that did not look like a puzzle. I felt irritated that I'd concocted such an image instead of grasping directly the specific puzzle or puzzles to which it might refer. Besides, my way of representing the puzzle seemed trite. Childish.

Suddenly, I was reminded of several puzzles with which I'd played as a child and then of one in particular that I never could put together. It was one of those difficult puzzles that had no picture on its surface. And recalling the frustration of trying often to solve that puzzle—a puzzle that did not look like a puzzle—I recalled a frustration over another kind of puzzle, a puzzle that was always clearly a puzzle. I recalled that when my parents wanted to exclude me from their conversation—or so I had reason to suspect—they would often break into a foreign language.

My thoughts then carried me back—or forth—to a moment in a play by Ibsen, a moment when a married woman who had consistently rebuffed the importunate advances of a would-be lover, now says as he's parting, "Au revoir." I remembered that on seeing the play I'd been impressed that Ibsen had conveyed the change in the woman's attitude not only through the content, "Au revoir," but through the switch in form, that is, the switch to French, the language of love. Looking back, I wondered why I'd been so sure that Ibsen's French was the language of love. At which point, I was startled to recall a similar sureness about the purpose of my parents' switch to foreign languages.

My thoughts then turned back to the analytical situation in which I'd seen my puzzle and to something my patient had said of a woman he'd met and found intriguing. I realized, as I'd not before, that his account—and intentions—had been unclear. I realized, too, that he had a habit of telling things in ways that at first seemed clear but later proved unclear. Which is to say, I realized, that he presented puzzles that did not (at first) look like puzzles.

Several weeks later, my patient became annoyed after I made a remark he found puzzling. In indirect association, he complained of a co-worker at his office who'd sent him an "ambiguous" note. I asked whether what I'd said, or some way I'd said it, had made him "uncomfortable." (Since "uncomfortable" was a euphemism of which I knew him to be fond, and since there were many familiar postural and tonal signs that he was in an embattled position, I thought it best to begin by heaping acceptable ambiguity on the already unaccceptable rather than begin with a more specific question or comment about his apparent distress.) He replied that he'd indeed been made uncomfortable. He said that as a matter of fact he'd been made somewhat "irritated" by my knowing so much about him and telling so little. It also made him "uncomfortable," he added, to tell of his irritation.

As we explored "uncomfortable" then and in later hours, it proved a euphemism for his anger and for the punitive fears his anger aroused. Later, "uncomfortable" more often proved an allusion to various "storms" of feeling and to his finding himself, in the face of those storms, un-comfortable: unable to be comforted. Whether "uncomfortable" referred mainly to the one or to the other—to signal or storm—was often unclear, another puzzle that did not at first seem a puzzle.

On another occasion, in after-the-hour reverie, my thoughts drifted back again to my patient's ambiguities and to his "uncomfortable" reactions to my ambiguities. And it occurred to me that, since I have an abiding affection for many forms of ambiguity, it was likely that my patient already had, and would have, many opportunities for such uncomfort.

Soon after, I began to see that when he was "irritated" with me for "keeping [him] in the dark," he kept me in the dark. One way was to tell a bit of what was on his mind, but not tell a lot, by which means he seemed both to give the devil his due and to take full advantage of chances to keep me, and himself, in the dark about what he later told me he regarded "dark" doings. Subsequently, he also told me he'd noticed that I often regarded a "point of ambiguity" in his associations as a good place to invite attention. Which invitations, he told me at last, he regarded as outrageous, since I could be as ambiguous as I pleased and he was expected to tell his reactions to my ambiguity; but when he was ambiguous I expected him—

"forced him"—to examine the reasons. This "point of ambiguity" and outrage led over time to his parents, who always "pried into" his secrets and themselves took the high moral ground of having no secrets to tell. Much later, what he called his "points of ambiguity" proved also to have several anatomical and psychosexual meanings.

Puzzling more about the many puzzles—my patient's and my own—to which my image of my puzzle had seemed in the first place to have alluded, or at least to have resonated, and in the second and third to have attracted my attention, I found myself thinking more about my own interest in and use of ambiguity—for better and for worse—in analyzing, painting, writing, and several other preoccupations. It seemed to me that in this proclivity I'd transformed myself from the one puzzled by the hidden meanings of my parents' words to the one puzzled by hidden meanings of others' words and, frequently, from the one puzzled by others to the one who puzzles. My thoughts then turned again—advanced or retreated—to other puzzles of my childhood: this time to puzzling fantasies and events of seeing and hearing my parents: fantasies and events whose outlines I imagine you can surmise but whose particulars I choose not to report. (I hope this choice reflects, mainly, an appropriate use of ambiguity.)

Nor was that the end of the puzzling reverberations. Several years later, with this same patient, another image of my puzzle came to me, and, associating after the hour to its details, I again recalled the puzzle without pictures that had frustrated me in my childhood. This time, however, I recalled that some pieces of that puzzle were darker and some were lighter, and the darker pieces did not seem to fit with the lighter, which led me back past the childhood wishes, excitements, frustrations, resentments, and fears of seeing and hearing to which I'd been pulled by my first seeing the puzzle and then, by an unexpected turn, to images of another puzzle: images of dark and ambiguous expressions of my mother. That puzzle of darks and lights was, I've since found reasons to believe, a puzzle that confronted me when, at an age young enough to rely more on puzzling pictures than on puzzling words—or moving between the one and the other—I was faced over several months with my mother's distressing departures from her ordinarily cheery demean: dark pieces, indeed, that did not fit with the bright.

I imagine you find this sample of self-inquiry too labored at some points, too facile at others, too full of everything, and not enough of anything. I imagine you find it hard to distinguish advance from retreat. And I imagine you wonder whether my visual images and related inquiries were useful in facing the analytical problems at hand or merely part of the problems.

If so, your problem is not, I believe, solely the consequence of my condensing and censoring my account for the sake of economy and privacy. If my best inquiries were fully reported under the best of circumstances, they would, I believe, strike you as replete with these and other deficiencies (just as your self-inquiries, I believe, would strike me). I feel sure that few analysts would be tempted to rank any of my self-inquiries—or yours—on a par with good-enough analytic hours, let alone with the proverbial best.

Still, for my part, when I first engaged in these inquiries, I was more impressed by their contributions than by their limitations. I want to say again what I said before: I think such initial excesses of satisfaction are one of the major occupational hazards of self-inquiry—I know they are for me. Looking back later, I was struck by the many screens within screens within screens. Memories of hearing my parents' puzzling shifts of language seemed to hint at and conceal memories and fantasies of hearing other things. Memories and fantasies of hearing things seemed to hint at and conceal memories and fantasies of seeing things, and memories and fantasies of seeing actual puzzles seemed to hint at and conceal memories and fantasies of seeing other puzling things. Puzzlings about how mechanical things fit together seemed to hint at and conceal puzzlings about how things anatomical fit together and in turn to hint at and conceal efforts to solve other puzzles—other and earlier mother puzzles. And memories of—or perhaps I should say re-memberances of—the earlier seemed to hint at and conceal memories of events and urges of the later. Contemplating over time such twists of my inquiries and similar twists in other inquiries–those of my own and of others–I began to see possibilities for further inquiry.

One thing leads to another and another. My self-inquiries seem to have followed the lead of the proverbial butterfly who, fluttering its wings in Peking–does it know it's now Beijing?–changes the weather in New York.

A panel on self-inquiry is a contradiction in terms. Self-analysis reported–or, as I prefer to call it, self-inquiry–is never quite the same as solo inquiry, just as journal entries reported are never quite the same as journal entries made solely for oneself. Nor do inquiries reported, or contemplated for report, stir the same after-inquiries. I single out this handicap for mention because I've found the most rewarding aspects of self-inquiry in the slow and long after-inquiry into the limitations of yesterday's inquiries. Indeed, I've come to regard it the main business of self-inquiry to trade yesterday's illusions for today's.

Though I cannot now manage a fresh inquiry into yesterday's inquiries, I want to outline a few directions in which my after-inquiries have led:

As I look back over the years at my inquiries into my visual images, my attention has been caught repeatedly by their simultaneously revealing and concealing nature and, in particular, by the frequency with which my associations have seemed first to head in one direction and then abruptly to dart off in another. In the case of my puzzle, for example, I was struck by the shifts from self to patient, patient to self, present to past, past to present, distant past to recent past, and recent past to distant.

Associating to these shifts–shifts both of content and of form (including tone, accent, rhythm, dialect, grammar)–I've tried to rediscover and expand what I'd experienced, or almost experienced, before, during, and after such shifts. Regarding, for example, the flow of my associations to my puzzle, I observed a shift from an attitude of curiosity toward my associations to one of self-criticism, a shift culminating in the halting comment "childish." And where, the first time round, my associations had led from "childish" to childhood puzzles, this time, "childish," and the critical tone in which I'd spoken it, led me to quite a different childhood event—one I cannot remember ever remembering before—in which "childish" was part of a painful scolding I'd received for explorations tried and things seen, which is to say, an event in which curiosity turned abruptly to criticism.

Such inquiries into my associative shifts have led me often and expectedly to familiar and unfamiliar fantasies, wishes, distresses, defenses, and other elements and compounds of my intrapsychic conflicts. But they have also led me often—and this has surprised me—to inclinations, distresses, and compensatory measures for which we usually find it useful to employ other models: models of tension management, self–object differentiation, self-esteem regulation, identity formation, and other developmental challenges. And they have led me increasingly to previously unrecognized quirks of my character that embrace these conflicts, tensions, defenses, defects, capacities, and incapacities in protean combination.

(Only recently has it occurred to me that this preoccupation with my associative "changes of voice" and their meanings is not entirely unlike my childhood preoccupation with my parents' "changes of voice.") Whatever the origins, this approach has, through no conscious intent, widened my field of inquiry into the specifics both of my latter-day conflicts and earlier events. Moreover, such inquiries into after-the-hour associations to my in-hour images have revealed increasingly detailed parallels between my patients and me, parallels I at first took to be the simple consequence of "putting myself in my patient's place," (if putting onself in another's place is ever simple,) but that, on more thorough examination, proved considerably less simple.

In the case of my puzzle, for example, on first seeing the parallels between my patient's "uncomfortable" feelings and those I experienced in imagining the search for lights in the darks of my mother's face, I took this to be just such a simple instance of resonant place-putting. But, on looking back at my recorded inquiries, I found that I'd over and over been searching for other lights in the darks long before there were any recognizable signs of similar preoccupations on his part. For example, months before, on looking at a tree with falling leaves – by this time I was accustomed to associating both to images formed in analytic hours and to direct perceptions in and outside the analytic situation – I had recorded in my journal a series of mournful observations about the loss of the vivid leaves of autumn as winter approached and had juxtaposed cheerful associations about the consequent advantageous broadening of view. Looking back over these and other associations, I found that over and over I'd been advancing and retarding inquiries into feelings and fantasies stirred by my edging up to my 60th year. And for these feelings and fantasies I'd later searched and found parallels in my patient, who was nearing, with some misgivings, his 30th. (I cannot here present the evidence that going on in me was an active process of inquiry as well as a relatively uninvited eruption of unconscious tensions, but I think there were unmistakeable signs of both and of their inseparability.)

Over time, after inferring, by what I consider relatively small leaps of inference, many such hidden inquiries unfolding in myself and my patients, and many such efforts on my part at matching elements of those inquiries, I've come to the view that these hidden, half-hidden, latent or protoinquiries are not the simple consequence either of conscious self-inquiry or of psychoanalysis, but of abiding universal inclinations to inquiry on which conscious self-inquiry and psychoanalysis rely and which each tries, by its own means, to assist. When things go well, self-inquiry and psychoanalysis join, I believe, preexisting, almost-but-not-quite recognized inquiries; aid in their advance; and stimulate and aid new inquiries. And I believe that when things go best in analysis, explorations of my patients' hidden inquiries advance those and my own, and explorations of my hidden inquiries advance my own and my patients'.

I regard such hidden but close-to-the-surface inquiries as expressions of unending struggles to bridge between inner worlds and outer and to advance resolutions of old conflicts, modifications of old arrests and defects, and redefinitions of self, and other phase-specific tasks imposed by the inquirer's ongoing development. Or, rather, I regard these almost-but-not-quite-recognized inquiries—activities both driven and driving—as reflections of the tension between inclinations to find new solutions necessary to growth and development and inclinations toward outcomes, old and new, that retard or obstruct development.

In any case, when I can glimpse in myself elements of the ongoing struggles and inquiries I'm trying to understand in my patient, and elements of both my patient's efforts and mine to advance and retard inquiries, my understanding seems fuller, and the timing and tone of my responses to my patient, somewhat richer. I find, that is, that I can better put myself in my patient's place when I can find, through persistent between-hours inquiry, the places within me that are to be put in my patient's place.

I no longer regard self-inquiry as an occasional adjunct to analysis or an emergency measure to temper occasional countertransference intemperances, but an ever-necessary preparatory measure to sharpen my analytical vision. And I find such persistent and provocative after-hour self-inquiries essential to attain, in-hours, the more fluid and more evenly hovering attention—that excited calm and disciplined abandon—necessary for good-enough participation in analysis and other activities I prize.

In turn, the shift from preoccupation with the sufficiencies of my self-inquiries to the insufficiencies has led not only to changes in the form and frequency of my self-inquiries but to related changes in my analytic approach to my patients. In particular, I've found myself, through attention to changes of voice and other markers, trying more and more to tune to and assist my patients' ongoing edge-of-awareness inquiries, which, when followed persistently (along with attention to my patients' and my own efforts to advance and retard those inquiries), usually lead to fantasies and other manifestations of antithetical inclinations we usually call "deeper." (How much these changes in my self-inquiries and in my analytic approach have reflected ongoing trends in our profession, and how much they have unfolded relatively independently, I have, of course, no way of knowing. One thing does lead to another and another.)

From time to time, I've been asked whether I "really" thought analysts could or should try so consistently to observe themselves and whether I "really" thought they could or should try so consistently to observe themselves observing their patients. My answer is "very little" and "no." I don't think much can be accomplished. I don't think that what can be accomplished must be accomplished. Some analysts, like some patients, seem to advance their inquiries more successfully with more consciousness and some with less.

Still, it seems to me that if more analysts who find self-conscious self-inquiry helpful were to tell more about their inquiries (form and content), if we were to develop a climate in which fuller telling and hearing were more possible, if we were to develop a greater tolerance for the insufficiencies of our own and each other's inquiries, if we were to explore ways of expanding self-inquiry's modest possibilities, if we were to analyze and be analyzed and supervise and be supervised differently with particular stress on recognizing and assisting ongoing inquiries—we might learn a bit more about the uses and abuses of self-inquiry, about the workings of the analyzing instrument and its relation to self-inquiry, about some aspects of solitude, inquiry, and creativity ordinarily obscured by the two-party emphasis in our theories and methods, and, above all, about the complex subjectivities in our seemingly simplest activities, analytic and other; all of which might help us a bit in our efforts to confront the distortions imposed on our views and methods by our ubiquitous myths of objectivity.

If, despite conscious intentions to confine my remarks to my own experiences, I've now intruded more than one hortatory note—or revealed a hortatory intent in what purports to be merely autobiographical—still, I want to remind you and myself of what Matisse replied when in his old age he was asked what he would do if he were a painter just starting out: "I'm not qualified to say." he said "It's the job of the young to plan the future."

AFTERTHOUGHTS

This previously unpublished paper was part of a panel discussion on "Self-Observation, Self-Analysis, and Reanalysis" that took place at a meeting of the American Psychoanalytic Association, New York City, December 1991 (Gardner, 1991b).

When my editor, Paul Stepansky, kindly suggested that I collect and annotate some of my papers, I was reluctant. Among other things, I was reluctant to face the large gaps I knew I would find between what I had written and what I would now, in the rereading, wish to have written. Nowhere is that gap more prominent than in this paper. Indeed, in the rereading, I have found it difficult to resist the temptation to rewrite rather than annotate. Still, for brevity's sake, I have tried to stick to a few afterthoughts.

My opening reference to Winnie-the-Pooh's wobbling spelling was, I believe, more germane than I knew. I meant it to characterize my efforts at self-inquiry but, in retrospect, it seems also to characterize this essay itself. In it, I said some things I wanted to say, but I failed to say much that I failed to recognize wanting to say. Similarly, my later remarks about my experience in looking back at the insufficiencies of my earlier efforts at self-inquiry might, if I had taken those remarks more to heart, have urged me to look back as consistently at the insufficiencies of my less directly self inquisitive writings.

"And Who Will Analyze the Analyst?" was written in the context of, and shaped strongly by, the tension between my enthusiasm and my skepticism about the possibilities of self-inquiry. That skepticism had not stopped me from carrying out

studies in self-inquiry and from reporting them with a dis-
avowed "Come on in. The water's fine." Still, by this time I had
become increasingly concerned about ways in which, and the
ease with which, an analyst's efforts at self-inquiry in the analytic situation can come a cropper and, in particular, ways in
which and the ease with which an analyst's efforts to place self-
observations in the service of a two-person analytical vision—
thereby developing an interpersonal-intrapsychic vision—can
come a cropper.

If I were rewriting this essay today, I would try more directly
to comment on some of the possibilities of mishap. That's easy
to say but would have been difficult to do since I was not yet
fully aware of the nature and degree of my concern about a
contemporary change in the wind. Where earlier it had seemed
that the possible means and utility of an analyst's self analytical
efforts were receiving too little attention, it now seemed they
might be receiving too much or, rather, that they might be
receiving too much uncritical acceptance.

Today I think I would stress, or at least mention, how readily
in the analytic situation the self-inquiries of the analyst become
primary and observation of the patient secondary. Today I
would say: looking in the mirror is a hazardous enterprise; an
analyst's well-tempered analytical hypochondriasis easily becomes runaway. In which case, what may have begun as a
laudable effort to overcome a one-sided focus on the patient's
psyche—a remote and detached focus by a remote and detached observer—may give way to a one-sided focus on the
analyst's psyche masquerading as an "intersubjectivist" vision.
In that case, one obstacle to a two-party intrapsychic-
interpersonal vision is easily replaced by another. I might also
acknowledge that the analyst's self-observation is easily coupled with sudden and unsubstantiated inferences about the
patient, inferences difficult to evaluate when the analyst's
observations of the patient are so thin compared with observations of self. In addition, a belief in the infallibility of a
one-party view is easily replaced by a belief in the infallibility of
a two-party view. Accordingly, objectivism banished becomes

objectivism returned, albeit under cover of a would be inter-subjectivism. Today, I might acknowledge more directly the difficulty of moving fluidly between a focus on the patient, a focus on oneself, and a focus on the play between. Today, I might raise more direct questions about how much such a vision can be attained within analytic hours and how much it may require afterhour efforts. Today, I suspect I might also address more directly a well-known hazard of the analyst's self-inquiry: what may begin as an effort to prevent the translation of countertransference attitudes into unseemly action is all too easily translated into a self-congratulatory means of rationalizing and facilitating unseemly action. (And perhaps I would, or should, acknowledge that it's a lot easier to observe these and other peccadillos in other analysts than it is to observe them in oneself.)

I believe my mention of my efforts to second guess my earlier self-inquiries was an effort to describe a struggle to confront these and other difficulties of self-inquiry, difficulties that, in this paper, I had put in the background but today would put in the foreground. None of which would deter me from ending up touting self-inquiry if by self-inquiry we mean an endless series of transient positions for subsequent reconsideration and for subsequent reconsideration of those reconsiderations. Today, if I were to rewrite this essay, I think I might give considerably more weight to the importance of ways and means of second guessing earlier inquiries and particularly of searching for the ways in which by opening one door to the interior we close another. And I think I would try to make more explicit the notion that insofar as one aim of an analyst's self-inquiries is to help him or her to assist self-inquiries of a patient, the persistent reexamination of the analyst's self-inquiries, and the persistent search for their contributions and limitations, might help the analyst to attain a fuller and potentially more respectful understanding of the possibilities and impossibilities of a patient's self-inquiries.

Chapter Ten

IS THAT A FACT?
Empiricism Revisited, or
A Psychoanalyst at Sea

In *The Man with the Blue Guitar*, Wallace Stevens (1993) says:

> They said: "You have a blue guitar,
> You do not play things as they are."
>
> The man replied "Things as they are
> Are changed upon the blue guitar."
>
> And they said then, "But play, you must,
> A tune beyond us, yet ourselves.
>
> A tune upon the blue guitar
> Of things exactly as they are."

On first reading these lines, I surmised that Stevens meant to portray subjectivity triumphant. I knew that when Stevens was a student at the turn of the last century his university was a battleground between rationalists – rational positivists – and romantics. Indeed Charles Eliot Norton, the art historian and Dante scholar, complained that at Harvard, "Contemplation is an unfamiliar practice." He wrote to Santayana, who was on leave in Italy, "The University is given over to facts. Come back soon to redress the balance." Knowing these facts of history and seeing the facts of Stevens's poem in that light, I surmised early on that Stevens had joined the struggle of the Romantics to "redress the balance."

I have since come to appreciate more fully, however, the difficulty of telling what a poet intends, especially what a poet intends as portrait of subjectivity triumphant and what as caricature, and, most especially, as self-portrait and self-caricature. I have come also to appreciate that the "they" whom Stevens portrays, whether to celebrate or caricature, cleave from start to finish to a vision of objectivity. They trade a search for "facts" gathered by a rationalist for a search for "facts" proffered by a romantic. They trade "facts" shaped by visions of the poet as "mirror" for facts shaped by visions of the poet as "lamp" (Abrams, 1953). And they embrace at last what they regard as a higher objectivity, the objectivity of the poet's subjectivity. That is, they trade a vision of "things as they are" for a vision of "things exactly as they are."

I assume that in meeting today to reconsider what we regard facts, we have not met to refire the ancient struggle between romanticism and rationalism, a struggle quite robustly advanced for at least several millennia without any assistance from us. I assume we intend instead to join in one of our periodic efforts to unite – that is, to ponder the unity of – the "one world" we seem so often determined to tear asunder. And I assume our goal is kin to the reunion to which we aspire when, having arbitrarily divided the field before us, we assert optimistically that psychoanalysis occupies the midground between, or fuses, the humanities and the sciences.

That is, I assume we struggle repeatedly to reunite what we

oppose repeatedly as the scientific and poetic imaginations. Proceeding from this and allied assumptions, I shall treat the question "What is a fact?"—"What is a clinical analytical fact?"—as an invitation to address a few of my own struggles to steer the always unsteady course between the Scylla of inductionism and the Charybdis of eurekaism.

I expect I shall illustrate, partly willy and partly nilly, that a fact is a fiction with a transient credibility and a passing utility. I expect I shall have no choice but to illustrate that the facts we gather depend on the nets we cast, that our nets are changed by the facts we gather, and that we are highly inclined to prize our nets and net catch—and to find convincing reason for such prizing (we call it evidence)—till we can bear to discover, if and when we can, that our findings are untrue, partly true, or, at best, part of a larger truth we failed earlier to discern. Which, I assume, is why, when we set out to play Columbus, we are more apt to find America than India.

On the third day of his analysis, a patient told a dream. He was, he said, a deep-sea diver, down deeper than he had ever been before. It was beautiful, he said, but he wondered if it was safe. There was a lot of murky stuff he couldn't make out. He worried especially whether, when he wanted to come up, the man on deck could be relied on to help him when he signaled his want.

He went on to say it was fuzzy in the dream whether he was one of those divers who wear a special suit with the weights that keep them down and the long tube that carries oxygen from a boat, or a scuba diver, who carries his own supply. He said the dream was strange, because he had never been in such a suit but he had gone scuba diving once and rather liked it, and if ever he went down again it would seem more natural to be a scuba diver able to proceed on his own rather than a diver in one of those suits. He thought then of persons who, with no equipment at all, dive into the depths for pearls. He added in passing that, the deeper the pearl divers dive, the more beautiful the pearls but the greater the risks to their health.

One "fact" I found highly convincing was that my patient was extremely anxious about beginning analysis. Struck by the mythic and near inexhaustible possibilities of his vision of an oceanic journey into the deep, and hoping to help him to speak more freely of both his hopes and his fears (yet wanting to give him – and me – room to move about), I surfaced and said, "It was beautiful down there, but fuzzy, murky, and strange, and maybe risky."

I could have said, "Perhaps you're concerned about the beauties and risks of analytic diving." I could have said, "Perhaps you're worried about whether you can rely on me." I could have called attention to his abrupt pause – a telling voice of silence – after he mentioned his preference for doing things "on [his] own." Or I could have invited him to dive more directly into one or another of the murky depths. I could have done any of these and more and done so in language nearer to secondary or to primary process. I could have said nothing. But I made the unremarkable remark, "It was beautiful down there but fuzzy, murky, and strange, and maybe risky."

To which my patient replied: "Oh. Well, I suppose I may be a bit worried about beginning analysis and whether I can rely on you."

For several weeks, he spoke repeatedly of the anxieties stirred by beginning analysis; his associations were replete with aquatic images suggesting fantasies of watery rebirth, of being swallowed up by forces inside and out (Jonah and the whale played a prominent part), and in particular, fantasies of the risks of his own and others' carnivorous urges. (In this context, he made passing reference to an old and repetitive dream of being like a rat and eating into, and therefore being engulfed by, a huge piece of cheese.) Other images suggested fears of being drowned in his feelings and fears of losing his bearings, his connections to others, and perhaps himself.

But he talked of these lively matters in an oddly flat way. He moved abruptly from one image to another, one subject to another, and what I took to be derivatives of one developmental era to another. Moreover, his language shifted frequently and abruptly from carefully crafted sentences, whose elegance bordered on the stilted, to fragments of sentences and of words bordering on nonsense. And though his symbolism generally seemed unusually transparent, the border between free association and loose was far from clear—all of which seemed to me "beautiful, fuzzy, murky, and strange, and perhaps risky."

Through all this, my patient would sometimes pause unexpectedly and offer an observation about something he had said. At one point, I was struck by a note of equivocation in his observation and was reminded of his earlier comment, "Well, I suppose I may be a bit worried about beginning analysis and whether I can rely on you." I took it to be a fact that he was using these equivocal explanations (many of them plausible) to avoid the livelier steps that might have made these explanations and other associations more persuasive and more likely to lead to fresh associations, feelings, and understanding. Shortly afterwards, I took it to be another fact that my patient's explanatory propensity served, and was served by, his highly developed capacity to anticipate where his associations might be leading and his knack of using that capacity to jump ahead while leaving his feelings behind. Later, I concluded that this defensive proclivity was closely related to a highly advantageous trait for which I had by then learned he was well known and highly respected in his profession: an advanced capacity for foresight.

Early on, I regarded it a fact that in his abrupt dives into the depths, on one hand, and his rising explanations on the other, my patient was mainly too asleep or too awake to promote or permit livelier regression. And I regarded it a fact—a regrettable fact—that he was using both his aquatic descents (his dives into the ideational depths) and his explanatory ascents precisely to that end: to avoid livelier, more fluid, and more creative regression. That much I thought I understood. And yet, I had a persistent hunch that what he was doing in this way with words was much less important than something he was doing without words. It was therefore most unsettling that I found myself unable to identify that wordless something.

Which was when I saw a visual image, an image that led me

to another hunch, a hunch so persuasive that I regarded it as both factual and pivotal. I saw an image of a toy with which I had played as a child: a small membranous-topped jar in which in an aqueous solution a glass figure descended and rose mysteriously in response to varying pressure applied to the top. I was reminded then of my patient's dream of the deep-sea diver and was struck by a contrast between the nature of the prime movers in his dream and in my image of the toy. In his dream, the diver had some degree of independence, however questionable, and, even if the man on deck had temporary control of the oxygen and ultimate control over the diver's ascent, there was at least the possibility that the man on deck could be influenced by the diver's wishes. But I gathered—and took it to be a fact—that in my image I had imagined myself fully in charge of the diver's descents and ascents as I had in my childhood been fully in charge of the movements of the figure in my toy. In short, I gathered that in my image I had toyed with my patient and, by that means, had tried to reverse what I now surmised to have been my patient's persistent mechanization of, and efforts to control, me.

Some might call my visual gambit a retaliatory tit for tat: a part objectification for part objectification. Others will have no trouble inferring other infantile aims, both erotic and aggressive. At the time, having by then made it a practice of paying particular attention to my in-hour images and of associating after hours to many, I inferred a mélange of such aims. A fuller account of those exploratory efforts (Gardner, 1983) would lead us too far afield. I do want to mention, however, that in my image of my childhood toy I found sufficient evidence to regard it as a fact that I was responding anxiously both to several conflictual urges and to several concerns about what I might find if I pursued more fully my studies of my visual images in this analysis and in others. And I then realized that in my attitude toward both my ongoing and my proposed explorations I was in a not quite acknowledged mix of anticipation and apprehension not entirely different from my patient's reactions to beginning analysis.

Having recognized these bits of previously unrecognized, or

at least not fully acknowledged, tension I began to feel a trifle less vexed and a trifle less perplexed by my patient's couch diving. And, soon after, it occurred to me that my speedy formulations about the defensive purposes of my patient's behavior, however accurate they might have been in some respects, included an effort to cope with my own anxiety— stranger and other—by imposing a mechanical conceptual model on my patient's doings and, in so doing, creating, as in my image of my childhood play, an illusion of being in charge.

Meanwhile, back in the consultation room, I began to put several other matters into what I took to be their proper places. By processes of which I am unaware, I concluded that, in his initial deep-sea diver dream, my patient had foreshadowed his vision of analysis more fully than I had appreciated. In retrospect it seemed clear that in his dream he had depicted analysis as a well-defined two-stage process: in the first stage, he explored the depths more or less on his own while I, at a considerable remove, tended or was the machinery that through a long tube supplied him with something called oxygen until on a signal from him I helped him in the second stage to resurface and to gain, or regain, a greater autonomy.

On first hearing his account of the diver dream, I had been impressed mainly by his manifest concern about whether I could be relied on to help him to resurface. But now, in the light of my image of the toy and of the meanings I had inferred, I took it to be a fact that he was concerned both that I might not be present in ways I should be present in the second stage and that I might be present in ways that I should not be present in the first.

Perhaps you have been wondering what I was doing all this time besides observing and inferring. Mainly, I was breathing. That may require a bit of explanation.

Somewhere in the third week of this analysis, I began to realize that when I spoke, my patient usually became agitated, and when I remained silent, he usually became calm; and those reactions seemed largely independent of the content and other recognizable aspects of my comments. And I began to realize that by dint of these and other reactions my patient was requiring of me a much greater economy of expression than I prefer. Indeed, he seemed mainly to want me to keep silent.

Which led me in turn to the view—I regarded it as another fact—that when my patient was particularly anxious he removed me from the role of coexplorer, and even of on-deck watcher, and assigned me another. That is, from changes of his posture, gesture, and breathing, and from several tangential comments about matters of oxygenation and respiration, I fathomed that in moments of heightened anxiety he would speak more softly, would listen carefully to my breathing, and would utilize the sound of my breathing (and a matching of his breathing with mine) to soothe himself. I also became aware that while speaking more softly he often spoke so rapidly and continuously that I was afforded only occasional opportunity to speak, which ensured that while I regarded myself as trying to understand him in the first place and to communicate my understanding in the second, I was in my enforced silence providing the "oxygen" for his loquacious somnolence and then by my speech, with its masking of my breathing, giving the signal for his abrupt and largely silent awakening. (Or, to be more precise, his brief pauses often called me to speak, and my speech often called him to awaken.)

Having become aware of these events of my unplanned artificial respiration, I was unsure whether they were mainly a primary effort at a dyadic respiratory union, mainly a replay of such union in preparation for separation (the two-stage image of his dream), mainly a retreat from other wished-for and feared dyadic unions or separations, mainly a retreat from other wished-for and feared early developmental engagements, or mainly a retreat from later tensions of later eras. I was also unsure whether any of my silences, comments, and questions were useful in any ways beyond those imposed by their effects on the rhythms and sounds of my breathing. Nor did I feel any sureness about any analytical possibilities of things to come.

At that point I might ordinarily have invited explicit exploratory attention to his anxiety and to the uses he was making of me. But a sense that my words would either have fallen on deaf ears or subjected him to unbearable anxiety led me instead to accept without comment what I inferred to be my preliminary (I hoped it was merely preliminary) assigned role. Shortly after which, toward the end of the first month, my patient's watery associations, his need for pulmonary pacification–and the watery pulmonary union it seemed to reflect–began to fade from view. Following which, my patient and I went on, with brief exceptions, to pursue a more conventionally collaborative analytic course in which our words and silences seemed to serve more advanced modes of discourse; some of those discourses were concerned with his occasional reversions to his elementary respiratory modes of tension management, but considerably more were concerned with other matters.

In the course of this relatively brief analysis–approximately six or seven years–I came to the view (I regarded this another fact) that my patient's initial reactions had been mainly a transient emergency response, an overdetermined faulting, so to speak, in which early dyadic events came to the fore and obscured temporarily the later and dominant triadic. I imagine some analysts would agree and others would judge that I had missed, or even scuttled, the boat.

But however much we analysts may differ regarding the depths–the distal events–we consider essential to explore, we differ still more, I believe, regarding the surface, the proximal events, from which we prefer to set forth on the way to the distal. It is to that choice of proximal events, a choice that strongly influences the directions of our subsequent soundings of the depths, and therefore of our fact findings, that I want now to invite attention. I want especially to invite attention to the ways in which the choice of where to begin reflects a never entirely successful effort to promote a relatively spontaneous unfolding of events rather than a forcing into the areas of our preference.

With apologies to those who find the familiar notion of surface and depth so fraught with confusion that it deserves to be scrapped, I shall try to describe one angle of vision I found myself employing repeatedly in this and subsequent analyses in addressing what I took to be the facts of what I took to be the surfaces from which we made our way to what I took to be the depths. As you try to follow my efforts, I anticipate your full agreement that it is notably hard to discuss the surface without seeming, or being, superficial.

I regard it as a fact that, having been challenged from the outset by my patient's protean moves, by his initial affective detachment, and by his seeming disregard for the meanings of words, I was stirred to attend with special care to whatever I could to help me to gauge what was most affectively lively or potentially so. I believe this challenge and stir played a large part in calling my attention to two sets of "facts."

One was a set of questions—partly *hidden questions*—that I found my patient pursuing repeatedly, questions that seemed both to organize and to be organized by his emerging tensions. From that perspective, I found his initial questions about what might happen if he were a deep-sea diver—and what could be expected of analysis and of me—one piece of a broad range of almost but not quite expressed questions *about the possible beauties and hazards, gains and losses, excitements and risks, and delights and disasters of entering into one or another imminent engagement.*

That set of covert questions led over time to a broad medley of unconscious tensions. Viewed from the perspective of libido theory, my patient's questions led to various erotic and aggressive tensions—oral, anal, and phallic. And viewed from the perspectives of other models, his questions led to dilemmas of tension management (pacification), affect delineation and modulation, differentiation and dedifferentiation of self and other, trust of self and other, self-esteem regulation and other increments of autonomy and at last, in triadic combinations, settled mainly and most intensely in and around oedipal configurations and their derivatives where the markings of well-differentiated intrapsychic conflict seemed central. (In this last context, for example, his propensity for foresight revealed itself to be interwoven with conflict-laden urges to look at sexual things hidden and with old anxieties about the consequences of looking where it was forbidden to look, of which the future was merely one "murky," though relatively acceptable, piece.) And it was in these largely oedipal configurations that transferential events eventually settled most consistently and proved most fruitfully to be analyzable.

The second set of surface "facts" that caught my attention particularly—the first being the ubiquity, power, and consistency of his hidden questions—was my patient's preference for advancing many of his hidden questions in a *particular genre*: a genre of verticalities. In his metaphors, dream images, and reports of stories in books, incidents in motion pictures, and everyday events, this stress on the vertical kept appearing in the form of vehicles going up or down, persons or animals walking, climbing, running, or jumping up or down, and things projected, pushed, pulled or lifted up or down. (My visual image of the ascending and descending figure in my toy, perhaps in resonance with his descending and ascending diver image in his dream, seems to have anticipated—or lined up with—these formal qualities.) And these rises and falls of persons, animals, and things were linked repeatedly to his almost but not quite explicit foresight-seeking questions about whether the going up or going down would lead to one or another pleasure or pain. In this context, going down in an elevator led to an early memory-fantasy of a homosexual experience; going up in an elevator led to a particular voyeuristic heterosexual configuration; going up in another elevator led to fears of going through the roof, flying off into space, and other mixes of Icarian fantasy with near manic "highs." Jumping up and down unsuccessfully on a pogo stick led to the memory of an adolescent experience of excitement and humiliation in which he phrased an invitation to intercourse as "How about some up and down?" rather than the colloquially correct "How about some in and out?" A television image of a man and a woman "going down" in an elevator led to a "joke" about "being blown" and to thoughts of "mouth to penis resuscitation." Watching a child slide down a hill on a sled led to a memory of childhood fears that he would get lost wending his way home after school. He recalled that he had developed the habit of taking exactly the same winding downhill route home each day and of taking careful note of landmarks along the way so that he could subsequently allay anxieties about getting lost both by watching for those landmarks and by imagining the landmarks to come. (Foresight, indeed.)

If it can be said that events settled at last into one affective configuration more than others, I think it a fact that, as the analysis proceeded, his up-and-down imagery and hidden questions led most often to the pleasures and risks of the rises and falls of his own and other persons' rage. In the course of that settling, rising, and falling, an event took place that I regarded as especially significant. One day, after I had made what I considered one of my very best interpretations, my patient paused for a moment and replied, "As Montaigne once said, 'No one is spared talking nonsense. The misfortune is to do it solemnly.' "

This was the first time he had expressed even such carefully muted displeasure with me. I considered it an indication of considerable progress. And I considered it an indication of even greater progress when, after quoting Montaigne, my patient said, with no help from me, that it was an accomplishment to say what he had just said but it would be more of an accomplishment if he could stop leaning on Montaigne and say what he had to say in his own words and say it more bluntly. Which he proceeded to do. Which ushered in many occasions when we were able to explore how a wave of anger toward me would lead him to make his dives into the depths or, alternatively, quickly to offer his characteristically equivocal explanations. All of which was followed over subsequent years by an increasing access to and tolerance of his previously unconscious rage, of his related fantasies and anxieties, and of his previously unconscious efforts to prevent the development, or at least the recognition, of those anxieties. All of which was accompanied by a markedly increased capacity for self inquiry into these and other areas previously inaccessible. Which was accompanied by a marked decrease in his conspicuous need to blur the differences between his own views and those of others, even when, or especially when, those differences were major.

One other event exemplifies developments during this time of his increasing access to his aggressive fantasies and affects and of his increasing willingness and ability to speak up. My patient recalled having read, during his adolescence, *Billy Budd*, with whose protagonist he had immediately identified. His version of that tale was that Billy was a young sailor whose sole and fatal flaw was that when enraged he became unable to express himself in words and so had no choice in the end but to express his rage toward his tyrannical captain by killing him. He added that these events contained allusions to contemporaneous American sailors pressed involuntarily into service and allusions to earlier American colonists, who, lacking a proper voice in their affairs, had no choice but to go to war.

Encouraged by the appearance in this tale of his telling juxtaposition of mutism and violence and by the welcome information that those in servitude had been preceded historically by those who had made war—another array of what I took to be analytical metaphorical facts—I passed up the opportunity to invite another round of analysis of his now familiar defenses. I asked instead if there was something for which *he* was at this very moment lacking a proper voice. (I assumed that he was pursuing several almost but not quite acknowledged questions of how to enter, and what the consequence would be of entering, another murky space: his rage toward several almost but not quite named tyrants.) I therefore took it to be another fact of progress when he launched without hesitation into a lively declaration of his resentment at having played "absolutely no part" in determining when I went off on holiday. This unfair arrangement reminded him of a number of parental doings from which he had been barred without possibility of complaint, still less of revolution; after which, he remembered a repetitive childhood fantasy of diving or being pushed down under water and of coming up cleansed of his devouring rage. In that context, I learned that he had been reared in circumstances alive with the imagery of Immersion Baptistry. Which suggested yet another (surface?) dimension to his initial deep-sea diving responses to embarking on analysis. Immersion, indeed. And a hope for a kind of salvation perhaps.

What I have presented here is not an analysis. It is a picture of an analysis. And it is a picture colored by the fact that I took it as fact that analytical events moved constructively toward what I took to be salient expressions—particularly in the transference—of what I took to be triadic reorganizations of the primarily dyadic events of the opening days of the analysis. Among those latter-day triadic events, I found what I regarded to be factual evidence that my patient's fantasies of mating with his mother included not only phallic wishes and fears but wishes for, and fears of, incorporation and fusion. And his wishes for and his fears of punishment from his father seemed to include both wishes for and fears of castration and wishes for and fears of being swallowed in toto by his father as a consequence of his own biting, and choking, rage. (In this context, he recalled that somewhere between ages four and five, he had experienced a brief series of asthmatic attacks.)

These perspectives—may I call them shared insights?—and the exchanges that went into their development proved of therapeutic advantage. And follow-up many years later suggested that my patient had gone on to attain significant expansions of that advantage. Nevertheless, since so many of yesterday's facts are today's ephemera, I have no reason to believe my patient and I would uncover today precisely the facts, and only the facts, we uncovered—that is, constructed—yesterday. And surely, if I were another analyst, I would uncover—that is, construct—other facts.

Some analysts would see my patient's initial dives as retreats from his primitive rage and from the guilt responsive to that rage. Some would see those dives, along with other of his off-putting activities, as direct expressions of that rage. Some would stress his incorporative urges, others, his competitive.

Some would see his move toward a regressive fusion as protective against a feared intimacy. Some would locate that feared intimacy as dyadic, some as triadic. Some would see his efforts to soothe himself with the help of the sounds of my breathing as largely a response to the sensory deprivations of the unfamiliar analytic situation or perhaps more specifically to my failures to offer sufficient support, guidance, interpretative assistance, evidence of my presence, or other. Some would see my initial irritation with my patient as a failure of empathy. Some would take that irritation as evidence of the depth of my patient's hostility. Some would be especially interested in his uses of activity to guard against his passivity, and vice versa. Others would follow and respond to much else. Which is simply to note the obvious fact that the facts we construct are inseparable from the theoretical and other subjectivities that go into our assumptions, observations, and conclusions.

If I had reported this analysis at greater length and in greater detail, and especially if I had reported more precisely who said what to whom and what happened when and to whom, we might be able to address the questions of saliency more effectively. We might. But I imagine you would agree that, even if in so doing I had managed to provide a stronger illusion of objective reporting and perhaps given you more useful information on which to arrive at independent judgments, my report would still have remained highly subjective, as would my choice of which analysis to present and which aspects to highlight.

To illustrate a detail of that last point, I want to mention something I have failed to mention about my reporting of the analysis in question. Not long after I wrote this report, I learned, with the help of modern medicine's most sensitive diagnostic instruments, that I was suffering from a hidden pulmonary disorder. At the time of my analytic reporting, therefore—which long followed this analysis but shortly preceded my receipt of the medical report—was the patient whom I reported as so attuned to my pulmonary functioning the patient about whom I was (consciously) reporting, or was it—

or was it also—I? We all know of patients' dreams that seem to have anticipated a bodily disfunction. This piece of my report of this analysis—my emphasis on my patient's attunement to my respiration—could be said in this regard to resemble, or be, a dream, a dream in the form of a report.

Still, even if I shall never be able to say precisely what is "blue guitar" and what are "things as they are," I take it to be one advantage of paying attention to my patients' hidden questions that I do not find myself, as often as I once did, playing exactly the same notes on exactly the same strings. Analyses have become less tidy. And I choose to see that untidy development as a fact of progress because I have found that following the lead of my patients' hidden questions (and the play between those questions and mine) has helped me sometimes and somewhat to temper my always ready inclinations to dive intemperately into one or another of the depths of my preference. I have found that following the lead of my patients' almost but not quite recognized questions has helped me sometimes to help my patients and me to explore both the surfaces and the depths that my theory and other predilections urge me to urge my patients to explore and sometimes has helped me to help them to explore some surfaces and depths that I suspect I might otherwise not have helped them to explore. That is, I believe that following the lead of my patients' hidden questions has helped me sometimes to find better meeting grounds between my patients' hidden questions and my own and accordingly sometimes to struggle a trifle more effectively with that inescapable disorder of aging theories and theorists that Jane Goodall called "hardening of the categories."

In suggesting that attending to my patients' hidden questions may have such partial and occasional elasticizing advantages, I hope I have not, despite my efforts to illustrate some of my subjectivities, seemed to espouse a naive theory of theory-free perception of hidden questions of the surface and, ultimately, theory-free perception of the depths. Few of us nowadays would choose (consciously) to espouse what Bacon prized as "pure perceptions" or what Nietzsche suitably

belittled as "doctrines of immaculate perception." Clearly I
have theories, even if not entirely clear theories. Clearly my
theories shape what I infer to be my patients' hidden questions.

Insofar as theory is concerned, especially one that guides
clinical interventions, I prefer a theory that invites my attention
now to the derivatives of one developmental era and now to
those of another, rather than a theory that invites my attention
consistently and persistently to one or the other. Whether I
have come to that theoretical preference mainly as a consequence of attention to patients' hidden questions or whether
that attention is mainly a consequence of manifest or latent
theoretical preference, I do not know. I do know that attention
to hidden questions has led me with different patients to what
I regard as derivatives of predominantly different developmental eras and has led me with many patients—perhaps
most—to what I regard as fluctuations among the derivatives of
one era and another before events have settled predominantly
into one or the other. And I believe (that is, I have a hunch) that
this habit of meandering over this broader characterscape has
resulted in a slightly greater therapeutic leverage than did my
work when, as a matter of principle and practice, I moved more
rapidly, persistently, and consistently to the analysis of the
derivatives of the particular era I then considered to be, with all
patients for whom analysis was appropriate, the predominant
era of choice. And I also have a hunch that attending to hidden
questions in the light of a longitudinal developmental theory
rather than a cross-sectional has helped me sometimes and
somewhat in my struggles to be guided rather than driven by
my theory.

I believe this preference regarding theory is in harmony with
my assumption that it is essential to try to identify the
epigenetic patterns now salient—not just epigenetic patterns
present—in my patient's psychological world. Which means I
assume there are such patterns organized in my patients' and
my psychological worlds, and I assume those patterns are
influenced by, but not the exclusive product of, the joint
subjectivities that come inevitably into play as I try with my
patients to identify those patterns. And by the same or a related

token I assume it is essential to scrutinize repeatedly as carefully as I can my own subjectivities as well as my patients'. I assume also that there is nothing unusual about these assumptions; I mention them simply to try to differentiate them from the assumptions of some analysts whose outlook in some other respects—for example, the need for the development of a mutually satisfactory language or narrative—resembles my own.

Nevertheless, even if I have reason to suspect that my approach has proved on the whole advantageous to my patients and me, I have reason to know that this approach is as eminently misusable as any other. I trust I need not count the ways. As Polya reminds us, "When you have satisfied yourself that a theorem is true, you start proving it."

What, then, is a clinical fact? Etymologists tell us that the word fact is derived from the past participle of the Latin *facere*, to do, and therefore means "something done or true." It might constitute better psychology (if poorer etymology) to say that the word fact is derived from the present participle and, therefore, means "something doing." A fact, after all, is not an homunculus that springs fully formed either from the events at hand or from our heads, but rather is a depiction, a transient depiction, of a perceived moment—a freeze frame—in an epigenetic process.

Informed and hampered by our theories and other preconceptions, we find—that is, construct—consistencies of content, form, and purpose. From the constructions we call observations, we formulate the constructions we call facts. And then, in slow but unending spirals of revision and in occasional transcending leaps that defy description but not imagination— modern mathematicians call them "combinatory play"—we construct and reconstruct larger and larger systems of facts. The evolution of our facts, therefore, is no less complex than the evolution of our species.

Whether such internally consistent systems are delusional or "truthful" and, if truthful, how useful for the aims at hand, are knotty questions of validation to be taken up elsewhere. But, knotty or not, the day comes at last when, having searched repeatedly for evidence of the correctness and incorrectness of the "facts" our patients and we have constructed, and having together become hopeful of the sufficient correctness of some of those facts, hopeful of the sufficient value of some of what has gone on between us in the course of our collaborative endeavors to uncover (construct) and correct those facts, and hopeful of the potentially abiding nature of some of our patient's expanded capacities, we find our patients and ourselves pursuing the knotty question—sometimes more hidden, sometimes less—of whether the analysis is finished. Which reminds me of a story:

Do you remember the Ruskin trial? Permit me to review the facts. Whistler had been commissioned to paint a portrait and had done so in his then-evolving impressionistic style. His patron was disappointed with the results and consulted the eminent Ruskin. Ruskin pronounced the portrait unsatisfactory because incomplete. He advised that payment be withheld. As a consequence, Whistler took Ruskin to court. Many learned experts were called as witnesses to address the question: When is a picture finished? At last, Whistler was called to the stand. He said, "The picture is finished my Lord, because I intend to do no more."

AFTERTHOUGHTS

This essay was first presented at a conference on "The Conceptualization and Communication of Clinical Facts in Psychoanalysis," London, October, 1994. It was subsequently published in the *International Journal of Psychoanalysis* (1994, 75:927–937).

When I was first invited by my London hosts to address the question "What is a fact?" (a clinical fact), I found it a question not only literally but figuratively from afar. On first consideration, I found it a question I was not especially eager to address. Nor did it help to be told that each participant had been chosen to represent a particular position. I did not know what position I had been chosen to represent, and, since my hosts seemed disinclined to tell, I did not think it cricket to ask. Still, on further consideration, I found it an invitation I could not refuse. Not the least of my reasons was that I hoped that in trying to answer the unanswerable question "What is a fact?" I might discover the position I was alleged to occupy. And I believe I did.

Now as I read the paper in the context of the other essays in this collection, I am struck that this factual question which seemed first to come out of the blue, was actually a question with which I had long been tussling, even though I had never put it so simply and directly to myself as it had now been put. Moreover, I am struck that my hidden answers to this, and closely related epistemological questions had long been shaping my changing analytical approach. Accordingly, the question seemingly posed from afar met my longstanding questions at least half way. And, similarly, the passing remark about my unnamed (and perhaps unnameable) position met at least half way my brewing if not fully recognized wish to take a reading on my "position." By the same token, the request that I offer a clinical instance to illustrate that position, coupled with unusual circumstances that allowed me to speak more freely than usual about a patient, stimulated me to offer more extended clinical excerpts than had been my custom.

So much for the context. Now a few details of the text and the subtext:

When at the outset I decided to take the question *What is a clinical fact?* as "an invitation to address a few of my own struggles to steer the always unsteady course between the Scylla of inductionism and the Charybdis of eurekaism," I thought I was referring solely to my struggles as a clinician. As I proceeded, however, my account carried me back repeatedly to events of my preclinical years. And what I had intended as a reference to a general tension between Romanticism and Rationalism—a tension in analysis and other fields—redirected my attention to several of my own "ancient" tensions between those very same polar pulls. I recalled, for example, several of my polar conceptions of poesis and science, several of my polar representations of linked aspects of my nature, and several of my polar childhood notions about the natures of my mother and my father, which, if I had known the terms, would have led me to designate my mother a Romantic and my father a Rationalist, thereby giving added, if not entirely needed, weight to my urges and efforts to oppose one to the other.

It seems to me now that "What is a Clinical Fact?" shaped by general references that proved personal and by personal references I hoped to be general, repeated and extended preoccupations and questions that had played hide and seek in my head from early years and that had found various forms in my writings over later years. Among the more clinical expressions was my aforementioned preoccupation with, and manifest and hidden questions about, the problems of attaining and maintaining a fluidity of psychoanalytic perspective and method. The clinical example in this essay readdresses that long-standing preoccupation by sketching some ordinary, and what I take to be necessary, shifts of stance: shifts, for example, between observations of patient and observation of self, between observations close to and observations less close to theory (and observations now close to one theory and now close to another), between observations of content and observations of form, between observations of forces we call external and observations of forces we call internal, between observations of what we call surface and observations of what we call depth, and between and among observations of many etceteras. In sketching those shifts I meant (consciously) to sketch a few bits of the process by which one temporary "truth"—one "fact"—repeatedly gives way to another, which is also to say, to highlight the "relational" nature of our representation of all we experience, including all we call "facts." In retrospect, however, I see that I was also choosing to redirect attention from the impossible question "What is a Clinical Fact?" to the almost-impossible question: what are the processes by which we arrive at what we are willing, perhaps eager, to call facts? And all this became an opportunity—or I insisted on making it an opportunity—to spell out something of what I had come to mean in referring to psychoanalysis as a joint, if often unrecognized, endeavor to advance (and to obstruct) the hidden questions of a patient and an analyst and the play between them. Looking back, I find it hard to tell how much it was the evocative nature of the question my hosts had posed that led me in the directions this essay went, and how much it was my stubborn addiction to my own hidden questions and to my expanding custom of answering other persons questions by replying "That reminds me of a story." Whatever the inner workings of the chance—in both senses of the word chance—I am most grateful to my hosts for posing the ancient, ever-present, and still impossible question: *What is a Clinical Fact?*

Chapter Eleven

FREE ASSOCIATION REVISITED

D o you remember the trial of the Knave of Hearts in *Alice in Wonderland*? When the White Rabbit is called to the stand, he asks, "Where shall I begin?" The king replies: "Begin at the beginning, and go on till you come to the end."

When, in one way or another, at the start of an analysis a patient asks what the White Rabbit asked, we analysts, in one way or another, reply as the King replied. For a century, we have honored that Alice-in-Wonderland-ish question and answer. "Where shall I begin?" "Begin at the beginning, and go on till you come to the end."

But why do we persist in this recondite practice? And why do we persist at a time when so many other means, chemical and other, are available for relieving our patients' distresses? Why do we assume that putting into words what one has never had a chance—or dared—to put into words and speaking those words aloud to oneself and another is likely to be useful in a fair number of ways to a fair number of persons willing to try?

What happens when our patients begin at the beginning and go on till they come to the end?

Analytical healing, like physical, is a highly mysterious process. Analytical healing, like physical, proceeds by pathways even more mysterious than the pathways of sickening. And no more evidence is needed of our deplorable ignorance than our habit of using the very same word—cure—to refer to the restoring of health and the pickling or smoking of fish. Yet, confused and confusing as our curative impressions may be, we do know that when one person tries to be honest with himself or herself and with another, many good things tend to happen. I shall try here to isolate one set of happenings that I believe are of special consequence and might be of more consequence if we paid them more attention both in the analytic and other situations in which one person is rash enough to try to come to the aid of another.

Last fall, I participated in a panel discussion of the question: What is a Fact? We may not have advanced any novel answers to that gnarled and knotty question, but I am grateful to have learned that Thomas Nagel once said: "*Every* view of the facts is a *partial* view from *somewhere*." The view of the facts I shall sketch today is especially partial. It's intended to highlight the human leaning toward self-inquiry and some consequences of trying to serve that leaning.

There's nothing new about the notion of a human leaning toward self-inquiry or, by the same token, about the notion that persons we call patients have leanings toward self-inquiry. It has long been recognized that "free" association is shaped by many intentions, some of them self-exploratory. But it's one thing to pay lip service to self-exploratory intentions; it's another to take them seriously. I believe we frequently give self-exploratory intentions more lip than attention; and even when we concede in the abstract that these play a significant part in organizing free association, that concession does not entirely free us from the assumption that our patients' self-exploratory intentions are largely the consequence of their assimilation of our own laudatory exploratory aims and means.

It's remarkable how hard it is to free ourselves of such

self-aggrandizing assumptions, assumptions close kin to the notion that a student's push to learn is largely the consequence of his or her teacher's push to teach. I have tried to address that pedagogical fancy in a recent series of essays (Gardner, 1994), and I shall not belabor it here. I mention this teacherly hazard, however, to accent my impression that no would-be helpers – teachers, analysts, body doctors, or other–have a monopoly on the tendency to underestimate the self-exploratory intentions of the persons they are eager to help.

When we become helpers, helpers of whatever stripe, much vigilance is needed to uncover and to temper our persistent assumptions–often self-fulfilling–that the exploratory intentions and practices of the persons we would help are mainly an aping of our own. When we become helpers, it's remarkable how quick we are to assume the missionary position.

We analysts, for example, pressed by importunate urges to look deeper, are apt to look past our patients' exploratory intentions. Real analysts always look deeper. Besides, like other troubleshooters–auto mechanics come readily to mind– we're in the habit of accentuating the negative; a common form of this analytical habit is to pay closer attention to patients' efforts to obstruct exploration than to their efforts to advance.

It might be thought that our neglect of exploratory intentions reflects the tried-and-true policy of not looking a gift horse in the mouth. But we are especially able to overlook our patients' hidden questions, just as teachers are especially able to overlook their students' hidden questions, because we are so inclined to focus attention on whatever we want our patients– or students–to learn and consequently, in our furor to help– whether to teach or to cure–so inclined to ignore what our patients and our students are *trying* to learn. (Our other reasons for taking so lofty and therefore myopic a view, I leave to your own experience.)

Obstacles notwithstanding, it's possible to observe that patients try often and persistently to advance exploratory intentions and, to that end, to pursue hidden questions, important questions, questions almost-but-not-quite asked, or, if asked, almost-but-not-quite acknowledged, or, if acknowledged, almost-but-not-quite taken seriously.

But if questions are important enough to advance, who would be trying only to advance them? Questions lead to answers that are welcome, to answers that are unwelcome, and to answers that are welcome in some ways and unwelcome in others. Patients, like their caretakers, try often—perhaps always—both to advance and to obstruct their hidden questions. We are all more adventuresome and stodgier than we know. Even the most avid inquirer, like Homer, occasionally nods.

Hidden questions take many forms. Some can be brought easily to awareness; some cannot. Some are kept outside awareness through inadvertent inattention and some through intentional inattention. Some questions are allowed easily into awareness but without full affective connections; some are allowed easily into awareness with full affective connections but without acknowledgment, and some with full affective connections and acknowledgment but severed from connection with systems of action.

Though the ebb and flow of hidden questions is usually easier to obsrve in the analytic situation, similar ebbs and flows of similar questions are often readily observable in other locations: casual conversations, formal speeches, talk shows, newspaper articles, books, motion pictures, plays, news reports, scientific reports, poems, paintings, lectures, and much else. What purports to be a disciplined or an undisciplined response to particulars of the moment often reveals, both within the analytic situation and outside, the organizing effects of the hidden questions of the person who engages those particulars.

Proceeding from the assumption that self-exploratory inclinations and hidden questions do not arise entirely from an analyst's ministrations or from spontaneous generation (undoubtedly Spallanzani would have been happy to hear that), I find it useful to assume that the free association method invites many of its progressive possibilities by fostering a climate in which patients can advance their preexisting hidden questions, can advance their inclinations to form new questions, can explore and temper their inclinations to obstruct those advances, and can expand their capacities to advance hidden questions, old and new, inside the analytic situation and outside.

The term hidden questions may suggest processes consistently linear, logical, and lexical. But "hidden questions" embrace inquisitive operations all along the border between the more linear, logical, and lexical and the less, and ranging from the latent to the incipient, the verbal and vocal to the gestural, and from the contemplative to the near-reflexive. "Curiosity" may be too general a name; "hidden questions," too specific. Exploratory processes often meander somewhere between the one and the other. I would not, for example, want to exclude from the company of hidden questions an infant's efforts to imitate the moo-moo of a cow.

I mention this bovine example because recently my one-year-old granddaughter, who had returned from an area where she had a chance to observe many cows, opened a fallen magazine to a picture that included, in one small portion, a herd of bison. The figures were so small as to be barely visible, but this did not stop her from saying at once what she had learned to say of cows: "moo moo." I take it she was pursuing an inquiry into the nature of a category of objects whose similarities seemed to justify designating them by the same name. That is, I take it she was pursuing the first task of scientific investigation and, for that matter, of the poetic imagination: the ordering of similar but not identical entities into categories that permit the making of useful forecasts, for example, the forecast that, when she hears the sound "moo moo," it signifies the presence not of a tree but of a cow. In her spoken answer to the silent question, "What is it that goes 'moo moo?'," she may not have arrived at the precise classifications she will later employ, but she has begun to raise "questions," hidden questions, essential to carrying her on her scientific or poetic way.

Looked at one way, hidden questions seem small. Looked at another, hidden questions, like those in my granddaughter's ingenious investigation, prove germane both to a narrow range of outer-world particularities—in this case, the mooings of cows—and to a network of inner-world strivings essential to the explorer's salient tasks of growth and development: in this case, tasks of classification and linguistic development and of communicating with, pleasing, and being pleased by parental and other persons. From that larger perspective of purpose and need, the hidden questions of one person reflect hidden questions that remain alive, in one form or another and to one degree or another, in all. And, though some hidden questions are especially timely in one of the "seven ages of man," no questions are ever answered once and for all. Through all ages, fresh variations on old questions arise again and again. Which is why, looked at one way, hidden questions seem small, and looked at another, grand.

Since the hidden questions of one person tend to resonate with the hidden questions of another, and since, in addition, the free association method and our derived analytical observations and theories have long been shaped and reshaped by the hidden questions of the patients who have attempted to tell all, and by the hidden questions of the analysts who have tried to listen to all, it ought not be surprising to find a frequent and fortunate overlap of the exploratory agendas of patients and analysts. In my work and that of colleagues, I have found this frequently and fortunately to be the case.

Perhaps you are now objecting that I began by complaining that we tend to ignore our patients' hidden questions and now I have claimed that the free association method advances our patients' hidden questions and our own and that I have even gone so far as to claim that the development of our analytic observations, methods, and theories has been guided—and by-and-large guided well—by the play of our patients' hidden questions and our own. Surely I cannot have it both ways; either we have paid sufficient attention to hidden questions, or we have not. Still, this seems to me one of those circumstances in which the answer lies somewhere in the middle. I believe we might do well to pay more attention to hidden questions. But I also believe that, despite our failure to attend to them more fully and despite our failure to give them the considerable credit they deserve, our free association method has served often to advance those questions—our patients' and our own—and served often to advance the play of those questions and our capacities for that play and interplay. That is to say, although at the front of our heads we have often, perhaps usually, been oblivious to patients' hidden questions and our own, the free association method has helped us often, at the back of our heads, to tune to and assist in the advance of those questions. (I leave it to those with a better knowledge of physiology and anatomy to state the cerebral locations more precisely.)

From observation of my own work and that of colleagues—colleagues of various persuasions—I have the impression that when we work well enough, whether we know it or not, we generally work in ways that advance both our patients' hidden questions and our own. (This is not to minimize significant differences between one practitioner and another but simply to stress significant similarities.) I have come to regard it a central aim and requirement of the free association method to advance the hidden questions of *both* patient and analyst and the play between them. I have tried to sketch a few fragments of that double play in a book called *Self Inquiry* (Gardner, 1989). Here, for simplicity's sake, I shall speak more of the questions of the patient and less of those of the analyst.

On the second day of his analysis, the first patient of the day, in telling of a recent event, and then in summary of a motion picture he had seen the night before, and then in description of a person he called "someone I know," appeared almost but not quite to be posing the question, Should I keep to myself, or should I try to make friends? and on the verge of posing the related question, If I make friends, how do I keep my freedom? (The identity of the possible friends, the meaning of freedom, and the risks of losing it were the subject of many hours to come.) The second patient's main hidden question revolved around, Do good ends justify bad means? (The particulars were not quite so abstract as my excerpt might suggest but not so concrete as they were later to become.) A third went on for most of the hour on, Is so-and-so a person to be trusted or feared? A fourth was vexed by, Am I being neglected or am I asking too much? A fifth edged around, What would happen if I told them all to go to hell? (In several ways, this question seemed to be edging toward questions about me.) A sixth was fascinated by, What would happen if I made a pass at my boss's wife? A seventh told a dream, spoke of an unhappy child, and mentioned a memory of his father that seemed to reflect the question, What can be done to cheer a person who is despondent? (This almost-but-not-quite asked question was couched in thoroughly altruistic terms; and not till much later did he give any hint that he considered the question relevant to himself except insofar as it might help him to help those—those others—he wished to help.) An eighth seemed on the verge of seeing that she was asking, or almost asking, What would happen if I gave you a present? (She seemed to know but not yet dare to say what present, nor did I think it yet timely to ask—or offer a guess about—the answer to the question she had so far almost but not quite asked.)

Given the superficiality of these interrogative details, you may now be posing the not-very-hidden question, So what? At least, I hope so. To offer a few tentative answers to this question, I have optimistically imagined you have almost but not quite asked, I shall try to sketch a few experiences and conclusions that I hope may pertain to dilemmas and challenges you may have faced, or may face, in psychoanalytical endeavors or in other endeavors in clinics, private offices, schoolrooms, home rooms, or other walled or unwalled places in which you may have tried, or one day may try, to exert a beneficial influence on one or another willing or unwilling person.

A Michael Polanyi (1958) reminds us that all knowledge, hard or soft, however reenforced and disguised by group assent, is personal knowledge. I hope you will forgive me if I now use that reminder as license to indulge briefly an elder's urge toward the autobiographical.

My recognizable concern with hidden questions began some 20 or 25 years ago when I decided to take a closer look at the play between my patients' free associations and my evenly—it might better be called unevenly—hovering attention. But my attention was not caught by hidden questions straightaway. I was too busy looking at visual images. That is, I found, and was surprised to find, that during analytic hours I was seeing visual images. Many visual images. And I found those seeings more than a bit unsettling because, being of conservative analytic and other origins, I had been brought up to believe that a person who saw things—especially who saw things repeatedly—was in deep trouble. In those circles, a person who saw things was held in about as high regard as persons who in earlier times were found worshipping graven images rather than the word.

Whether because of or despite these grave misgivings, I soon began associating after hours to the visual images I remembered having seen during hours. I think I was trying to convince myself that seeing things was no more harmful or woeful than dreaming. But I found small comfort in these endeavors since I soon realized I had added to the habit of seeing things a habit that was at least as questionable as talking to myself.

Still, I persisted. That is, the habits of seeing things and talking to myself persisted. And it was these habits that brought hidden questions to my attention. My associations to my images revealed many of my longstanding tensions, conflicts, and remedies, along with many hidden questions relevant to those tensions, conflicts, and remedies, and revealed many variations lively in my reactions to the patients in whose presence I had concocted these remembered-and-associated-to images. Before long, my images and associations began also to bring to my attention analogous hidden questions of my patients, and I could not help seeing ways in which my patients and I were *trying repeatedly both to advance and to obstruct our hidden questions* and ways we were managing repeatedly to advance and to obstruct our own and each other's.

Analysts have frequently shown a warm preference for Horatio Alger stories, especially for those in which the hero or heroine analyst departs temporarily from his or her customary purity of volition and vision till, having diligently subjected his or her transient aberration to self-inquiry, he or she deserv-edly—and usually speedily—overcomes adversity and reaches higher planes of personal development and analytic accom-plishment. A reader of one of my own Algerish writings once warned me that I seemed to have forgotten Oscar Wilde's warning: "Only the shallow know themselves." I have since tried my best not to add to the store of those stories, and I hope I shall not appear to be failing miserably in that determination if I now elaborate on my belief that my efforts at self-inquiry—especially with respect to my visual images—have here and there helped me to observe the play of my patients' hidden questions and my own, and here and there helped me to put these observations to what I consider to be useful analytical ends.

The first ends seemed narrowly technical. Tuning some of my comments to some of my patients' hidden questions—sometimes directly, more often indirectly—seemed to help my patients to explore what I had come to expect patients to explore and to do it a trifle more effectively. In that regard, both the content and form of their hidden questions proved useful. I found that each patient had his or her favorite modes or genres of inquiry; and even a rudimentary grasp of those genres or modes helped me here and there to couch my comments in language that seemed to help my patients to advance their hidden questions.

One patient, for example, proceeded over and over in the manner of a story teller of everyday events. And when his hidden questions were most pressing, it was his habit to advance those questions through prolonged description of each person he had met that day. Usually those persons were many. He would tell what each said and how each said it. When he really got going, he would mimic what each said and how each said it and would even accompany his verbal and vocal mimicry with the appropriate gestures. I thought at first that he was merely making small talk. And sometimes he was. But it turned out that he used this particular brand of small talk as much to advance as to obstruct hidden questions. Often, having gone on with his reports of the day, and having imitated one and another person successfully, he would grasp that his imitations were not merely imitations; the person he was imitating was also him. In this sense, his efforts to take distance from his own traits by describing and imitating those of another often allowed him to sidle up to what was too charged to approach more directly.

Another patient was accustomed to dwell at length on the vagaries of the weather. Sometimes he would talk in vivid particulars about storms, floods, hailstones, tidal waves, electrical activity, and the like. Sometimes he would talk in lofty abstractions about high-level west to east currents, Arctic and Canadian airflows, Greenland turbulences, seasonal conditions in faraway places, etc. etc. (And there were many et ceteras.) The vivid particulars would often lead to hidden questions; but the tepid abstractions seemed more often to lead away from or to obscure emerging questions. When I was able to use lively enough, but not too lively, meteorological metaphors, these seemed, on the average, to help him to advance his hidden questions.

Later, one determinant of his penchant for weather reports became clear. It turned out that in childhood he had been accustomed to awakening his doting grandfather each morning by telling him about the day's weather. It also turned out that one of his frequent hidden questions (especially prominent in his questions about me) was whether various persons were asleep or awake and, if awake, whether they would respond with boredom or as his grandfather had. He described grandfather's response with what he characterized as an untranslatable word: "qvelled." Though something may have been lost in the translation, I gathered from what my patient said and from the way he said it that, when awakened and told the weather, grandfather invariably both quivered with delight and swelled with pride. But what proved considerably more untranslatable than the word was the reaction itself, a reaction that my patient tried frequently and unsuccessfully to translate from past to present. And those efforts and their mainly unhappy consequences stirred and were stirred by many of his hidden questions and left him often with the feelings that the persons to whom he turned were nothing but fair-weather friends.

Another patient, when his associations and hidden questions were most vigorous, described various persons, places, and things with meticulous attention to their appearance, especially to colors, and most especially to warm colors. One day, he said he had met a woman who was fascinating; but she did not sound fascinating. When he went on to say that she was a hot number, she still did not sound fascinating. But when he amended that by saying that she was a red hot number, the temperature in the room began rapidly to rise. And when, having earlier learned of the importance of his color scheme, I asked "Red?" his associations led quickly to a woman named "Red," then to many hidden questions connected with fantasies centering on body parts to which "red" led.

In this sense, I regarded commenting or questioning in harmony with hidden questions as a way to help patients to travel by their own royal roads from surface to depth, That is, proceeding from the familiar notion that everything is metaphor, I took the small extra step of treating hidden questions and preferred genres of inquiry—weather, colors, and the like—as especially metaphorical. And I found my patients' hidden questions leading often to unconscious erotic and aggressive urges, wishes, fantasies and their derivatives, unconscious distresses to which these gave rise, and unconscious ways of avoiding or tempering those distresses. Which does not seem remarkable since intrapsychic conflict topped my exploratory list. Also, since I was especially attentive to derivatives and reworkings of the oedipal era of development, it does not seem remarkable that hidden questions led my patients and me repeatedly to tricornered tensions.

Early on, hidden questions proved of added use in the analysis of transference and defense. I found, for example, that transference analysis went easier and deeper if I called attention to transference reactions not only when they were lively, convincing, tolerable, and accessible, but when they promised to be of particular interest to my patients. And I found that a good clue to the potentialities of heightened interest was the centering of patients' hidden questions on something they had observed about me, and especially something I had said or failed to say, or done or failed to do, on that very analytic day. Tuning comments to patients' hidden wonderings about such ongoing doings and misdoings and related questions about the nature of our relationship—actual, wished for or feared—often led more satisfactorily into the analysis of transference than comments unresponsive to, or at odds with, such questions. And proceeding where patients' hidden questions pointed the way seemed to make me a bit less prone to those interventions Anna Freud called "funneling everything into the transference" and Kenneth Calder has called "What about me?" interventions.

I found also that defense analysis generally went better when, having gotten a sense of the thrust of hidden questions, I tried to help my patients to see ways in which, and reasons why, they had been trying ingeniously both to advance and to obstruct those questions. And I found it helpful to restrict myself, when I could, to calling attention to obstructive inclinations and the reasons for them, when those inclinations seemed most clearly opposed to the (hidden) explorations the patients had only moments before been trying to advance. I believe this policy of focus and timing often helped me to avoid proceeding as if it were I alone who wanted to pursue a particular line of inquiry and my patient alone who wanted to obstruct. Predictably, some patients still found my efforts at defense analysis obnoxious or otherwise unacceptable. Still, things seemed to go somewhat better—I imagine you would agree that "somewhat better" is all that an analyst can hope for—when I did not provide extra incentive for patients to see my efforts at defense analysis as bellicose. And, sometimes, helping patients to see ways in which they were struggling *both* to advance and to obstruct their exploratory inclinations seemed both to encourage more effective defense analysis and to help in the discovery of other ways in which my patients were, like the rest of us, men and women both for and *against* themselves.

Although, at the outset, following the lead of patients' hidden questions seemed merely a way to reach familiar terrain—a handy adjunct to timing and tact—I gradually realized that my patients and I had begun to wander into terra incognita. Relatively incognita. But I soon found hidden questions leading—and leading often—to unexpected variations on what I had learned to expect, and leading increasingly to what I had not yet learned to expect. In particular, I found hidden questions leading to derivatives and reworkings of a much broader array of developmental happenings than, as a dedicated oedipalist, I had earlier expected. I interpret that to mean that following the lead of hidden questions helped me to engage in a little more exploration and a little less application, or at least in a little more fluid mixes of the two.

In any case, if the advances of hidden questions could be charted in a visual image, that image might be an upwardly expanding spiral; if auditory, it might folllow the course of a Gregorian chant. Characteristically, a small hidden question is advanced tentatively, then disappears, and then reappears as a larger question that includes but transcends the earlier.

These unfoldings usually proceed slowly; sometimes, however, they advance unexpectedly rapidly. It's hard to find words to describe the unexpected rapidities. At the risk of seeming to embrace an unseemly mysticism, I borrow from the humanities the familiar phrase transcendental leaps. (I dare not speak of epiphanies.)

In both content and manner of motion, hidden questions support the notion that analysis offers a chance at a second adolescence; it offers, that is, a chance at a second adolescence for those who have gone through a first and a chance for a first for those who in passing from childhood to adulthood appear to have skipped a first. Among resemblances between unfoldings of hidden questions in analysis and unfoldings of events of adolescence are 1) the alternations between slow and accelerated reorganizations of outcomes of earlier eras, especially reorganizations of oedipal reorganizations of outcomes of earlier eras; 2) the far-reaching expansions of grounds of, and capacaties for, self-inquiry; and 3) the heightening of capacities for creativity, mainly the creativity of everyday life, but occasionally creativity that seems larger than life.

In addition, the forward motions of hidden questions in the analytic situation, like many developments of adolescence, are often preceded by sudden loosenings of stable habits and by transient returns to habits long abandoned and to heightened preoccupations with old questions and old answers. These moments of loosening, backing, and filling are often unsettling to my patients and to me. Yet in these moments, patients have often proved ready to advance hidden questions, old and new, and poised to advance associated growth. And in these moments what we have said or done, and what we have failed to say or do, has often proved of more than usual consequence. Moreover, when patients have been able to face with increasing equanimity a series of such unsettling moments, they often show themselves more able subsequently to do so both in the analytic situation and elsewhere and more able to edge their hidden questions—and the challenges and dilemmas of which those questions were part—toward more creative outcomes. Accordingly, I have come to think of these unsettled and unsettling moments—these stutter steps—as moments of opportunity: opportunity for my patients to advance their hidden questions and creative capacities and opportunity for me to help them in those endeavors and to study a few steps in my patients' and my regress in the service of and in opposition to progress.

I want now to return briefly to the notion that, although the free association method offers special opportunities to help patients to advance their hidden questions, some help may not be impossible elsewhere.

Alistair Cooke tells of a visit to a physician to complain of a bad case of itchy ankles. His physician examined him carefully but was baffled. Cooke talked on. I don't know whether the physician helped him to talk on or whether Cooke managed to do so without help or despite obstacles. He seems a determined talker. At any rate, one thing led to another till Cooke suddenly recalled that before his rash appeared he had been hiking in the Nevada desert to get a sense of what the Forty Niners had gone through. And then, having remembered that, he suddenly appreciated that he had realized his aim all too well. He remembered that he had once read in the journal of a Forty Niner that those hardy persons often came down with something they called "alkali itch." Informed by this information, Cooke's physician gave him an appropriate ointment and the rash cleared up within a few days.

It might be regarded sufficient that Cooke got a chance to prove the old truism "No one knows better where the shoe pinches than the wearer" and so managed to find an answer to his manifest questions about his itch. But he may also have gotten a chance to advance his hidden questions. Precisely what those questions might have been—besides the narrowly ankular—we have no way of knowing. But in the light of Cooke's well-known efforts over many years to tell of his own "westward ho" from England to America, we might suspect that, by his efforts to secure relief for his ankles, he may also have been trying to advance questions about the broader consequences of following in the footsteps of one's predecessors. If such was the case, the remembrance of his desert exploration may have helped Cooke both with his ankle itch and his itch to advance other explorations, physical and metaphysical, his own and those of others.

Occasionally, even the most narrowly focused psychologist or physicalist stumbles upon surprising unities within the psychological world, within the physical world, and between the one world and the other. I suppose these unities seem so surprising because so often we work so hard to carve one world into many. As Shelley said in his *Defense of Poetry*, "Reason respects the differences, imagination the similitudes of things."

Among the similitudes to which the imagination is readily drawn by the to-and-fro motions of hidden questions are the happenings not only of adolescence but of other eras. Moments of opportunity highlighted in the analytic situation by attention to hidden questions—moments of loosening and backsliding—resemble the epigenetic nodal points described by many researchers in child and infant development. T. Berry Brazelton has described these as "touchpoints": moments when infants and children undergo dedifferentiations and sometimes regressions that, however unsettling to themselves and their caretakers, are necessary preliminaries to further growth and development.

And these *moments of opportunity* in individual history—whether in childhood, in adolescence, or in the advances of hidden questions in the analytic situation—might remind us of larger creative moments of social history, moments such as Bronowski (1978) described in *The Common Sense of Science* when he said of the late 17th century, "That was the time of change, *the hanging moment of instability* in which men like Cromwell and Newton could change the world." (The hanging moment of instability!)

In another context, in *The Ascent of Man*, Bronowski (1974) wrote: "Nature—that is, biological evolution—has not fitted man to any specific environment. On the contrary . . . he has a rather crude survival kit; and yet—this is the paradox of the human condition—one that fits him to all environments." To which might be added, one that requires the unending disorganizations and reorganizations, and the unending pursuit of hidden questions, possible to humans and necessary to that fitness.

In the physical world, the imagination is easily drawn to similitudes between the slow evolutions and abrupt reorganizations of hidden questions and those circumstances in which, after a series of slow and steady changes, one added change of apparently identical nature leads abruptly and inexplicably to a striking change in the nature of a physical entity: water becoming colder and colder till it suddenly becomes ice, or warmer and warmer till it becomes steam; or, as Alfred Marguelies reminds us, when the proverbial camel, after one last straw, becomes the victim of a broken back.

From still another view – a microscopic view – of the physical world, the disorganizations that precede reorganizations of hidden questions might remind us of the Nobel-Prize winning studies of Ilya Pregogine, who showed that even at the low levels of organization of elementary physical matter, movements toward lower levels of complexity are not inevitable end points; some moves downward pave the way for reorganizations at higher and more complex levels. (It may be helpful to remember in dark times that three laws of thermodynamics are insufficient and, in rosier times, that not all development is upward and onward.)

Clearly, there's more to analysis and to the free association method than the advance of hidden questions. To attempt a partial view does not commit us to a "part for the whole" view. Nor do we need to mimimize therapeusis if we acknowledge that there's more to analysis – and life – than therapeusis. I have tried here to invite you to consider the notion that the free association method, when it works well enough, helps people to advance their hidden questions and to enhance their capacities to advance hidden questions; which advancing and enhancing tends to expand awareness of previously hidden workings of the mind and heart; which advancing, enhancing, and expanding tend not only to alleviate disorder – to promote the resolution of conflicts and correction of dysfunctions – but to strengthen capacities for creativity, and therefore to enrich a life.

I have tried also to invite you to consider the possibility that whether you are one kind of psychological healer or another, one kind of physical healer or another, one kind of teacher or another, or some other person intent on helping someone to learn something or other, you might find it useful to gear your efforts – some efforts – to the hidden questions – some hidden questions – of the person you are intent on helping. If you set out to help someone to advance his or her hidden questions, and therefore to help yourself to advance your own, you may find yourself filled with an increasing respect—dare I say reverence?—for the complexities of conscious and unconscious functions of the mind, the unities of surface and depth, and the many ways in which hidden questions span, shape, and are shaped by the immediate events of what we call the exterior world and the timeless events of what we call the interior. And if you set out to assist the advance of hidden questions, your own and another's, you may find that, having begun with Lewis Carrol's "Begin at the beginning and go on till you come to the end," you will come at last to T. S. Eliot's (1968) "We shall not cease from exploration; and the end of all our exploring will be to arrive where we started and know the place for the first time."

AFTERTHOUGHTS

"Free Association Revisited" was presented as the Robert M. Gilliland Lecture at the Baylor College of Medicine, Houston, March 1995. It was intended for an audience of analysts and other persons engaged in what some call expectantly (and increasingly wistfully) the "helping" professions and others call equally expectantly (but I believe more brashly) by those business-driven terms the "managing" or "health-providing" professions.

This essay collects and restates the perspectives that emerged in earlier essays, shifts a few stresses, adds a few pieces, offers a few samples of hidden questions and genres of inquiry, touches on a few consequences for analytic procedure, connects the press of hidden questions in the analytic situation with similar presses in the world beyond, and then draws parallels between some aspects of these events of the psychological world and some aspects of events of the physical, thereby attempting a broad reach from particulars to panoramas. In writing of these matters in "Free Association Revisited," I was aware of being moved to invite members of the anticipated audience to turn attention in several directions – the analytical clinical, the pedagogical, the medical-physical, and the more global. I thought I was moved in this multidirectional fashion because of the mixed nature of the audience. In retrospect, however, I am inclined to think that this essay bears strong marks of my having reached a stage – some might say reached an age – at which some persons feel the urge to map where they began, where they have gone, and what they have seen, and then to discover (or devise) ways in which some things in the small world observed may belong to, or be placed in, a larger. Perhaps this is also to say that some persons, having begun at the beginning and gone on till they come nearer to the end, feel obliged to discern a few ways in which they have arrived where they started.

Looking back at this essay and the previous ten, I am struck once again by how often what I experienced at the time as specific responses to the agendas assigned or selected now appear transient responses to – variations on the theme of – a few abiding preoccupations and questions. I now assume that such unending weaves of current and old musings reflect both the organizing effects of our abiding preoccupations and questions and the spurring and bolstering effects that come of having chosen in the first place – *if* we have had any choice – an occupation that allows us (even encourages us) to pursue those very same agendas we are, however unwittingly, most determined to pursue. When our occupations are chosen in this fortuitous fashion – and are accordingly experienced as callings – our hidden preoccupations and questions may, with a bit of additional good luck, correspond to and correspond with some preoccupations and questions of some other persons in our chosen, and therefore calling, occupations.

REFERENCES

Abrams, M. H. (1953), *The Mirror and the Lamp: Romantic Theory and the Critical Tradition.* London: Oxford University Press.

Barron, J. W. ed. (1993), *Self-Analysis: Critical Inquiries, Personal Visions.* Hillsdale, NJ: The Analytic Press.

Berger, J. (1980), *About Looking.* New York: Pantheon Books.

Brazelton, T. B. (1992), *Touchpoints.* Reading, MA: Addison-Wessley.

Breuer, J. & Freud, S. (1895), *Studies on Hysteria.* 2. London: Hogarth Press.

Bronowski, J. (1974), *The Ascent of Man.* Boston: Little, Brown.

_____ (1978), *The Common Sense of Science.* Cambridge, MA: Harvard University Press.

Eliot, T. S. (1968), *Four Quartets.* New York: Harcourt Brace.

Fenichel, O. (1941), *Problems of Psychoanalytic Technique.* New York: Psychoanalytic Quarterly.

Gardner, M. R. (1965), On psychiatry and other schooling. In: *Psychiatry Education Today,* by I. Hendrick. New York: International Universities Press, pp. 99–108.

_____ (submitted), *Chez Pierre.*

_____ (1984a). Apres. (From) Au-dela du temps des seances. *Etudes Freudiennes,* No. 24. Paris.

_____ (1984b), To be (or not to be) an analyst. Presented at Psychoanalytic Institute of New England (PINE).

_____ (1984c), Analysis and self-analysis: Looking two ways at once. Discussion of Vann Spruiell's "The Analyst at Work." *Internat. J. Psycho-Anal.,* 65:39–44.

_____ (1987), Recollections. Panel on Sexuality, Neurosogenesis, and Analysis. Presented at meeting of American Psychoanalytic Association, Chicago, May.

_____ (1994), *On Trying to Teach.* Hillsdale, NJ: The Analytic Press.

_____ (1989), *Self Inquiry.* Hillsdale, NJ: The Analytic Press.

_____ (1991a), The art of psychoanalysis: On oscillation and other matters. *J. Amer. Psychoanal.Assn.,* 39:851–870.

_____ (1991b), Self-observation, self-analysis, and reanalysis. Panel discussion at meeting of American Psychoanalytic Association, New York City, December.

_____ (1994), Is that a fact? Empiricism revisited, or a psychoanalyst at sea. *Internat. J. Psycho-Anal.* 75:927–937.

_____ (1995), Free association revisited. Presented as the Robert M. Gilliland Lecture at Baylor College of Medicine, Houston, March.

Hendrick, I. (1965), The analyst at work. In: *Psychiatry Education Today.* New York: International Universities Press, pp. 99–108.

McCord, D. (1980), *Speak Up: More Rhymes of the Never Was and Always Is.* Boston: Little, Brown.

Polanyi, M. (1958), *Personal Knowledge.* New York: Harper Torchbooks.

Polya, G. (1954), *Mathematics and Plausible Reasoning.* London: Oxford University Press.

Rosenfeld, I. (1993), *The Strange, Familiar, and Forgotten.* New York: Vintage Books.

Spruiell, V. (1984), The analyst at work. *Internat. J. Psycho-Anal.,* 65:13–30.

Stevens, W. (1993), *The Man with the Blue Guitar.* Somerset, UK: Knopf.

Tolstoy, L. (1966), *Resurrection,* trans R. Edmonds. New York: Penguin.

Weinshel, E. (1990), How wide is the scope of psychoanalysis and how solid is its structural model: Some concerns and observations. *J. Amer. Psychoanal. Assn.,* 38:275–296.

Whitehead, Alfred North (1929), *The Aims of Education.* New York: (Macmillan) Free Press.

INDEX

Abrams, M. H., 141
Alger, Horatio, 171
Analytical healing, 163
Affect, 104–106

Barron, J., 74
Berger, J. 70
Brazelton, T. B., 178
Breuer, J., 79
Bronowski, J., 178

Calder, Kenneth, 174
Carrol, Lewis (Charles Lutwidge Dodgsen), 180
Chiaroscuro, 127
Clark, Kenneth, 49
Clinical psychiatry, 11–12
Clinical theory, 89

Cooke, Alistair, 177
Countertransference, 82, 117
Creativity, 72–73, 178–179

Defenses, 66
Deutsch, Helen, 87–88
Diagnostic interview, 14–15
Dreams, 38, 39, 71, 124–125, 142, 155
   analysis of, 125, 143
Dreamlike states, 39, 45, 65, 70, 71, 84, 124, 155
Duality, 106
   See also Polarity
Dynamic psychiatry, 15, 17, 18, 19–20

Education, psychiatric, 16–17,

50–52
Eliot, T. S., 180
Epigenetic
  patterns, 156
  nodal points, 178
  Eroticism, 85, 173

Fact, 142, 157–158,
  159–161,163
Floating attention, 35–43, 45
Fenichel, Otto, 100–101, 103,
  119–120
See also Oscillation
Fitzgerald, Scott, 94
Franklin, Benjamin, 73
Free association
  method, 46, 82, 165–166
  self-inquiry during, 55–61
  shifts, 133–134
  therapeutic value of, 79–80,
    95, 167–168, 179
  use of after analytic hours,
    35–41, 130–133, 170–171
Free attention, 114–117
Freud, Anna, 174
Freud, S., 38–39, 79, 104–106,
  125
See also Affect; Idea

Gardner, R., 18, 33, 35, 46, 53,
  60, 82, 97, 119, 137, 145,
  164, 168

Hendrick, Ives, x, 10–19, 90
Hidden inquiry (hidden
  questions) 134–135, 150–153,
  155–161, 164–181

Idea, 105–106
Ideals, departures from, 25–30,
  43, 44, 45, 74
Imagination, 72

Interpretation, 61
Introspection, 60, 73

Knowledge, redistribution of,
  63–65, 68–69

Lewin, Bert, viii
Lewis, Nolan D., ix
Linguistic development, 167

McCord, David, 101–102
Mimicry, 172
Mixed motive, 25
Monomania, 81
Multiple consequence (mixed
  consequence), 23, 25, 30

Nagel, Thomas, 163
Neurogenesis, 77–99
Neutrality, 23
Norton, Charles Eliot, 141

Objectivity, 96, 141, 154
Observation, 10, 13–15, 138,
  157, 171
Oedipus Complex, 90–93,
  149–150, 153
Oscillation, 100–121; See also
  Fenichel, O.

Passivity, 154
Perception, 47, 70–73, 116,
  155–156
Perspective, 153–154
Polanyi, M., 170
Polarity (polar play), 102–121,
  160
Pregogine, Ilya, 179
Progressive-regression, 71, 72
Pseudoanalysis, 13–14
Psychiatry
  as a science, 18, 114–115, 118

as an art, 18, 114–115, 118, 119
Psychoanalysis, 22
Psychosexuality, 130

Rado, Sandor, viii
Rationalists, 141, 159–160
Regression, 56, 124–125, 128, 144, 154
  adolescent, 92–96
Regressive-progression, 93
Representation, 72–73
Research
  psychiatric, 11, 12–13
  interdisciplinary, 11, 12

Romantics, 141, 159–160
Rosenfeld, I. 47
Ruskin trial, 158

Self-analysis (self-inquiry), 21–33, 57–61, 82–83, 122–139
  therapeutic value of, 66–75
Self-exploration, 163–181
Self-portrait (self-caricature), 141
Sensory deprivation, 154

Sexuality, 89–99, 173
Shakespeare, William, 101
Shelly, Percy B., 178
Spruiell, V., 31
Stevens, Wallace, 140–141
Subjectivity, 96–97, 141, 154, 157

Tartakoff, Helen, xi
Transference, 107–108, 153, 174
  analysis, 105–106
Twain, Mark (Samuel L. Clemens), 39, 78

Unity, 106, 141, 147–148, 177–178

Visual images, 45, 126–133, 144–145, 170–171
Voice, change of, 61, 63, 133, 135

Weinshel, E., 118
Whitehead, Alfred North, 9
Wilde, Oscar, 171
Wordsworth, William, 70, 101

Zetzel, Elizabeth, xii

For Product Safety Concerns and Information please contact our EU
representative GPSR@taylorandfrancis.com
Taylor & Francis Verlag GmbH, Kaufingerstraße 24, 80331 München, Germany